Spell Well

50 prescriptive spelling activities
for the primary and intermediate grades

Roberta A. D'Ambrosio

Virginia Strock

Marget Zographos

Fearon Teacher Aids
Carthage, Illinois

Editors: Bonnie Bernstein and Carol B. Whitely
Designer: Paul Quin
Illustrators: Mary Ann Schildknecht and Joyce A. Zavarro
Cover designer: William Nagel

ISBN-0-8224-6455-1
Printed in the United States of America.

1.9 8 7 6

CONTENTS

THE WHY AND HOW
OF *SPELL WELL*

Some children learn to spell easily, while others seem to have persistent and even painful problems mastering this basic skill. As resource specialists and teachers of learning handicapped children, we have been asked by many classroom teachers how they can help those children to whom spelling comes hard. Our answers and our general approach to building spelling skills are set forth in this book.

Spell Well's activities are geared for use in the primary and intermediate grades. Primary activities are appropriate for those children who have up to third-grade level skills; intermediate activities are for those with up to sixth-grade level skills. Activities throughout the book are designated for the primary or intermediate level and also for group or individual (one child with one adult) use.

Our first step with a chronic poor speller or spellers (and the first step we recommend to you) is to examine the errors the child or the group is making. You can do this by collecting samples from the children's work, samples which contain numerous spelling errors. Then compare the errors to those shown in the Diagnostic Chart on page 3. You will probably be able to match most of the individual errors to one of the five groups of examples. If one error seems to fit two categories of examples, categorize it as both.

The category to which you've matched the largest number of errors tells you which chapter's activities to use first. Those activities will help to strengthen the *related skill* you see in the chart and begin to reduce the frequency of that type of error. Later, refer back to the other types of errors the children made and begin to work in activities from the other corresponding chapters. Note that all these skills work in combination. Many of the activities may strengthen more than one skill for a particular child, and therefore the distinctions between chapters cannot be perfect. Activities have been divided in the most usable way we could devise; but feel free to mix activities, especially as you become more sensitive to the children's errors and skill weaknesses.

Chapter activities are structured in an easy-to-follow, step-by-step format, and all supplies and necessary preparations are noted. (You may want to have a tape recorder on hand for use with auditory activities.) For some activities, we have provided variations, and you may want to add others. Feel free to add to and adapt the activities to meet your particular students' needs.

Many of the activities require the use of a worksheet. In such instances, we have provided MAKEMASTER duplicatable pages for you. These are individually coded for use at either the primary or intermediate level. The

activity and its MAKEMASTER page have the same identification number for easy reference. We encourage you to use these pages just as they are or as models for your own worksheets, which may include words from your own spelling lists or the Chapter Word Lists we provide. Whenever possible, we have designed the activity worksheets so that the children may check their answers themselves, but where this has not been practical, you will have to provide an answer key.

A Glossary of Terms is also included for your reference. Definitions or illustrations have been provided for any specialized language or terminology used in *Spell Well*.

Please note that it is essential for the children to know the sounds of individual letters and be able to blend these sounds into words before they attempt any of the activities in this book. It is also necessary that they be able to read and understand the meanings of the words they are asked to spell. If the children you will be helping have mastered these tasks, then you are ready to use *Spell Well*.

DIAGNOSTIC CHART

Examples of Spelling Errors		Related Skills
Word	Child's Spelling	
mat	bsl	**SOUND-SYMBOL CONNECTIONS**
science	skwf	When errors are this severe, you must first teach letter sounds and blending (see p. 1).
desk	deks	**SEQUENCING**
was	saw	Strengthen with activities in Chapter One.
perhaps	prehaps	
first	frist	
people	peopel	
business	buisness	
children	childern	
animal	aminal	
does	duz	**VISUAL MEMORY**
sure	shur	Strengthen with activities in Chapter Two.
watch	woch	
where	were	
because	becuz	
enough	enuf	
pig	qig	**POSITION IN SPACE**
bad	dab	Strengthen with activities in Chapter Three.
pet	get	
guilt	quilt	
enough	euough	
have	hawe	**VISUAL DISCRIMINATION**
fell	tell	Strengthen with activities in Chapter Four.
oat	cat	
join	*join*	
fell	*feel*	
attack	*attach*	
train	chain	**AUDITORY DISCRIMINATION**
enter	inter	Strengthen with activities in Chapter Five.
thin	fin	
February	Febuary	
surprise	suprise	
equipment	equitment	
remember	rember	

CHAPTER ONE

BUILDING SEQUENCING SKILLS FOR SPELLING

Sequencing, in relation to spelling, refers to the ability of an individual to recall letters and letter sounds in the correct sequence to spell a word. Sequencing is therefore a memory function which has to do with remembering the spatial and auditory relationship of one letter to another within a word.

In the English language, which has an unusual number of irregular spellings (spellings in which letters do not correlate with actual sounds), it is important that children master visual sequencing skills. Otherwise, they will evidence chronic spelling problems that cannot be compensated for by other skills.

It is important to distinguish between problems of visual memory and problems of visual sequencing. When a child is trying to spell a word and his or her *visual memory* skills are weak, the child may rely only on the recall of the sounds within the word and fail to revisualize the whole word as a unit. The result is a phonetic misspelling, for instance, *laf* or *laff* for *laugh.*

Children with weak *visual sequencing* abilities have a different problem—they are usually able to recall the presence of phonically irregular letters in a word but are not able to remember the order in which they occur. The result is a sequential misspelling of the word, for instance, *lauhg* or *laghf* for *laugh.*

It is also common for children who demonstrate visual sequencing errors to missequence whole words (*saw* for *was, who* for *how*) which, when rearranged, spell other real words. Words with diphthongized vowels (*thier* for *their*) and word parts such as *le* and *el* (*appel* for *apple; camle* for *camel*) create visual sequencing confusions as well. In order to be successful spellers, these children need enough exposure and practice with commonly missequenced words so that eventually they are able to store and recall the words as whole units.

We have observed that children with weak *auditory sequencing* ability often misspell words which contain the more ambiguous sound combinations, such as a vowel plus the liquid consonant *l* (*culb* for *club*) or a vowel plus the liquid consonant *r* (*frist* for *first*). Sometimes these children will missequence letters which have similar sounds, such as the nasals *m* and *n* (*aminal* for *animal*).

The activities presented in this chapter are intended to give children with all of these types of sequencing difficulties practice in focusing on the internal sight and sound structure of words. This practice will help them develop a keener awareness of how the spatial and auditory organization of the letters within a word relate to its spelling.

5

1

COMPARE AND SEE
Primary or intermediate grades
Individual or group

Activity

Students determine whether the sequence of letters within two words presented to them is the same or different.

Preparation

Duplicate MAKEMASTER #1 for the appropriate grade level and give one copy to each child. If you prefer, make up and duplicate a similar worksheet using words from your own spelling list or the Chapter Word List on page 19. It is important for you to present the correct spelling of the word in column 1.

Procedure

1. Have the child look at the first column and notice the correct spelling of the word.
2. Then, have the child look at column 2, compare this word with the one in column 1, and decide if the words are the same or different.
3. If the word in column 2 is the same as the word in column 1, the child puts an *S* in column 3; if it is different, the child puts a *D*.
4. The child then traces the word in column 1 and writes it in column 4.

MAKEMASTER 1: PRIMARY

Compare and See

Name

1. Correct spelling	2. Same or different?	3. S/D	4. Write it
saw	was		
stop	spot		
card	card		
from	form		
left	left		
won	won		
how	who		
name	name		
left	felt		
sag	gas		
snag	sang		
tap	tap		

MAKEMASTER 1: INTERMEDIATE

Compare and See

Name

1. Correct spelling	2. Same or different?	3. S/D	4. Write it
under	undre		
head	haed		
kite	kiet		
become	boceme		
storm	strom		
farm	farm		
babies	babeis		
trunk	trunk		
friend	freind		
about	abuot		
teach	teach		
bright	bright		
goat	gaot		
fifty	fitfy		

2

CAN YOU TELL THE DIFFERENCE?
Primary or intermediate grades
Individual or group

Activity

Students first read and spell aloud a word which has commonly misse-quenced letters. After a time lapse, they rewrite the word.

Preparation

Provide each child with a copy of a spelling list featuring words which appear similar (no nonsense words), such as those listed in the Chapter Word List on page 19. Prepare a wall chart which corresponds exactly to the spelling list. Be sure that the same spelling words are listed in the same order. Hang the chart at the back of the room. Duplicate and distribute MAKEMASTER #2.

Procedure

1. First, have the child read the words on the spelling list aloud to you.
2. Then have the child go to the posted wall chart and look at the first word.
3. The child then says the word and spells it aloud.
4. Then the child returns to his or her seat and writes the word.
5. Ask the child to compare this written word with the word on the spelling list. If an error has been made, have the child repeat this procedure until the word is spelled correctly.
6. Then the child goes on to the next word on the list.

Variation 1. For additional reinforcement, you may ask the child to practice each word a designated number of times.

Variation 2. For a group activity, put each word on an individual card large enough to be seen by all the children in the group. You can say a word and then flash the card (1 second per letter). Remove the card, wait for 10 seconds, and then give the children a signal to write the word.

MAKEMASTER 2

Name _____

Can You Tell the Difference?

1.	
2	
3.	
4.	
5	
6.	
7.	
8.	
9.	
10	
11.	
12	
13.	
14.	

1. clam
2. feel
3. calm
4. fell
5. how
6. spot
7. who
8. now
9. stop
10. own

Wall chart

1. clam
2. feel
3. calm
4. fell
5. how
6. spot
7. who
8. now
9. stop
10. own

Spelling list

3

MATCH THE BOX
Primary or intermediate grades
Individual or group

Activity

Students first trace over all the letters of a word, and then they fill in the letters missing from each of several partial representations of that word.

Preparation

Duplicate MAKEMASTER #3 for the appropriate grade level and give one copy to each child. If you prefer, make up and duplicate a similar worksheet using words from your own spelling list or from the Chapter Word List on page 19.

Procedure

1. Ask one child to say the first boxed word on the worksheet. Have all the children repeat the word together. Then have each child trace the letters of the word in the box.
2. Next, have them fill in the missing letters in each partial representation which appears directly below the boxed word.
3. Have the children self-check their work by tracing the word they have written and the boxed word. Have them compare them to see if they are correct.
4. Have the children go on to the next word in the column. They should complete all the words in the column before going on to the next boxed word.

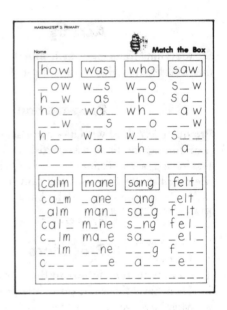

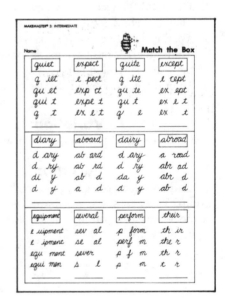

MATCH THE ORDER
Primary or intermediate grades
Individual or group

Activity

Students first trace the word presented to them and then find a matching word which they must trace and rewrite.

Preparation

Duplicate MAKEMASTER #4 for the appropriate grade level and give one copy to each child. If you prefer, make up and duplicate a similar worksheet using words from your own spelling list or from the Chapter Word List on page 19. Provide the children with brightly colored markers.

Procedure

1. Have the children trace the letters of the first spelling word in column A.
2. Ask them to look at the other words in column B and find the word that matches the one in column A.
3. Have the children trace the letters of the matching word.
4. Then have them write the word in column C.

Variation 1. Have the children circle the word in column B that is the same as the one in column A instead of tracing it.

Variation 2. Have the children cover the word in column A after they have traced it and choose the correct match from memory.

MAKEMASTER® 4 PRIMARY

Name _____ Watch the Order

A	B			C
won	now	own	won	
tub	but	tub	ubt	
dog	god	dog	gdo	
girl	girl	gril	glir	
was	saw	aws	was	
eat	ate	eat	tea	
farm	fram	famr	farm	
who	who	how	ohw	
name	mane	name	nema	
clam	calm	clam	clma	
there	there	theer	three	
left	felt	letf	left	
stop	stop	spot	sopt	
tap	atp	tap	pat	

MAKEMASTER® 4 INTERMEDIATE

Name _____ Watch the Order

A	B			C
spread	spraed	spread	sapred	
forward	froward	forwrad	forward	
introduce	introduce	intorduce	intrdouce	
section	section	sectoin	seciton	
brief	breif	brief	brife	
listen	listne	lisetn	listen	
anxious	anxoius	anxious	arxious	
awful	awful	afwul	awufl	
fifth	fifeh	fitth	fihtf	
ought	uoght	ought	ougth	
fabric	fabirc	fabric	fibrac	
quiet	quite	quiet	queit	
perform	preform	perfrom	perform	
except	expect	execpt	except	
probably	porbably	probably	probalby	
several	several	sverael	serwal	
dairy	dairy	diary	draiy	
bread	beard	bread	braed	
abroad	aboard	abraod	abroad	

5

WORD CUT-UP
Primary or intermediate grades
Individual or group

Activity

Students cut apart the letters of a printed spelling word and reassemble them in the correct sequence.

Preparation

Duplicate MAKEMASTER #5 for the appropriate grade level and give one copy to each child. If you prefer, make up and duplicate a similar worksheet using words from your own spelling list or from the Chapter Word List on page 19. Provide each child with a pair of scissors.

Procedure

1. Have the children cut off the answer key on the heavy line and turn it face down.
2. Ask the children to say the first spelling word on the word list and then cut apart the boxes for each letter of that word.
3. Tell them to turn the letters face down and mix them up.
4. Have them turn the letters over and place them in the correct sequence to spell the word.
5. Then ask them to check and correct their spelling using the answer key.
6. If the word is spelled correctly, they should go on to the next word. If an error has been made, ask them to correct it before continuing.

Variation 1. To make this activity easier, have the children look at the answer key as they reassemble the words.

Variation 2. To make this activity easier, you can instruct the children to color-code the trouble spots before cutting the words apart.

Variation 3. Use the above activity as a game by having the children give their cut-up words to a partner who then reassembles the words.

Variation 4. Instead of having the children correct their work individually with their answer keys, have one child reassemble the word on a pocket chart in front of the group. Then ask the rest of the children to check their spellings with the word in the pocket chart.

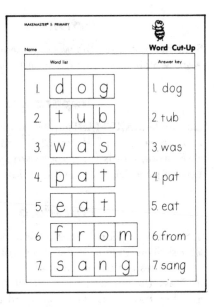

6

MAKE THE SENTENCE
MAKE SENSE
Primary or intermediate grades
Individual or group

Activity

Students must discriminate between two similarly appearing words within the context of a sentence and then write the correct choices in the blanks provided.

Preparation

Duplicate MAKEMASTER #6 for the appropriate grade level and give one copy to each child. If you prefer, make up and duplicate a similar worksheet using words from your own spelling list or from the Chapter Word List on page 19. Make sure that the two words offered as choices in each B sentence consist of the same letters but in a different sequence. Each child will need a pencil and a colored marker. (It is important that the point of the marker be thin enough so that the letters are not distorted when written by the child.)

Procedure

1. Have the children look at box 1 and read sentence A aloud.
2. Then have them use the colored marker to trace over each letter of each circled word while spelling the word aloud.
3. Next, have them look at sentence B and find the word that is the same as the first circled word in sentence A. They should then trace each letter of that word with their markers while saying the letters aloud. Then have them cross out the incorrect word.
4. They should do this for all of the words in sentence B which correspond to the circled words in sentence A.
5. In sentence C, have the children write the correct words in the blanks with pencil.
6. Have them check to make sure that all three sentences are alike.

MAKEMASTER 6: PRIMARY

Make the Sentence Make Sense

Name _____

1) A. The (clam) is (on) the (shore).
B. The clam calm is on no the shroe shore.
C. The ____ is ____ the ____.

2) A. See the (little) (girl) (read).
B. See the littel little gril girl read raed.
C. See the ____ ____ ____.

3) A. Look at (their) (blue) (desks).
B. Look at thier their bule blue desks dseks.
C. Look at ____ ____ ____.

4) A. (Eat) (four) (apples) now.
B. Eat Ate fuor four apples appels now.
C. ____ ____ ____ now.

MAKEMASTER 6: INTERMEDIATE

Make the Sentence Make Sense

Name _____

1 A. You must (usually) be (quiet) in a (hospital).
B. You must usually usually be quite quiet in a hospital hospital.
C. You must ____ be ____ in a ____.

2 A. There are (probably) several (good) (performances).
B. There are probalby probably sevreal several good performances performances.
C. There are ____ ____ good ____.

3 A. That (fabric) (ought) to make a (nice) (spread).
B. That frabic fabric ought ought to make a nice spread spread.
C. That ____ ____ to make a nice ____.

4 A. The (fifth) (section) should be (brief).
B. The fifth fifth sectoin section should be brief breif.
C. The ____ ____ should be ____.

5 A. (Listen) to the (train) and climb (aboard).
B. Litsen Listen to the trian train and climb abroad aboard.
C. ____ to the ____ and climb ____.

6 A. (Expect) the (dairy) to have new (equipment).
B. Except Expect the dairy diary to have new equipment equipment.
C. ____ the ____ to have new ____.

7

ALPHABET CARD SPELL
Primary or intermediate grades
Individual or group

Activity
Students spell a dictated word by putting together letter cards in the correct sequence.

Preparation
Use words from your own spelling list or from the Chapter Word List on page 19. List all letters the child will need to spell each word dictated. Make a set of cards cut to uniform size for each child and put one letter on each card. Give each child one complete set of letter cards and a blank card large enough to cover any word made. Each child should also have a paper and pencil. Prepare one set of large cards for yourself with one of the words written on each one.

Procedure
1. Tell the children what letters they will need for the first word. Give the letters in random order. For example, for the word *third*, you might say, "Put the *d*, *i*, *t*, *r* and *h* in front of you."
2. Next, show your large word card to the children and say the word *third*. Then say the sounds *th-ir-d* in isolation.
3. Now remove the card, repeat the word, and ask the children to place their cards in the correct order to spell the word.
4. Then hold up your large word card and ask the children to make sure their word matches yours. Give them time to check and correct.
5. As a final step, have the children cover their word with the blank card and write the word on their paper. Then ask them to uncover their word made from letter cards, check, and correct their word.

Variation. To make this activity more difficult include several letter cards which the children will not need to spell the word in the group of letter cards they put in front of them.

Child's cards

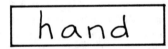

Teacher's card

8

ONE-LETTER-AT-A-TIME SPELLING BEE
Primary or intermediate grades
Group

Activity

Students in a group take turns calling out the next correct letter of a dictated spelling word and then write the entire word.

Preparation

Have ready a list of words from your own spelling list or from the Chapter Word List on page 19. Each child will need a pencil and a piece of paper.

Procedure

1. Say the first word, use it in a sentence, repeat it, and then have the children say it aloud.
2. After the correct first letter has been offered by a child, repeat that letter and then the word.
3. Call on a different child for the second letter. Continue this procedure until the word is correctly spelled.
4. If an incorrect letter is given by a child, ask the child to listen while you repeat the word with the correct letters up to that point. Then have the child try again.
5. When the complete word has been correctly spelled by the group, ask the children to write the word on their papers. Then ask one child to spell the whole word aloud as the others check and correct.

Variation. To make this activity easier, do it as above, except as each correct letter is given by the children, instruct them to write that letter.

9

BODY SPELL
Primary or intermediate grades
Group

Activity

Students spell dictated words in proper sequence using letter or syllable cards.

Preparation

Use words from your own spelling list or from the Chapter Word List on page 19. Make a set of white tagboard cards large enough to be seen from the front of the room for each spelling word on the list. A set should consist of separate cards for each letter (primary) or syllable (intermediate) in a word. Print each letter or syllable boldly in black. Make enough additional red and green blank cards so that every student has one of each. Each child will also need a piece of paper and a pencil.

Procedure

1. Pass out the first set of cards to the children. If there are four letters or syllables in the word, four children will have a card.
2. Spell the first word aloud or say each syllable.
3. Ask the children with the cards to come to the front of the room and position themselves in the correct sequence to spell the word, holding up their cards for the rest of the group to see.
4. Spell the word aloud again.
5. Have the children who are still at their seats hold up their green card if the word has been spelled correctly or a red card if it is incorrect.
6. If an error has been made, ask the children to reposition themselves in the correct sequence.
7. Then ask the children at their desks to write the word on their papers and check their answers by looking at the cards held by the children at the front of the room.

10

COUNTDOWN
Intermediate grades
Individual or group

Activity

Students identify the number of syllables in words dictated by the teacher.

Preparation

Have ready to dictate a list of words from your own spelling list or from the Chapter Word List on page 19. Each child will need a piece of paper and a pencil.

Procedure

1. Say the first word, stressing each syllable separately.
2. Ask the children to repeat the word as they clap out each syllable.
3. Tell them to write the number of syllables down and then write each syllable separately. Teach or review the rules of syllabication if necessary.
4. Write out the correct syllabication of the word yourself on the board. Have the children check and correct their answers.

11

FIND THE HIDDEN LETTERS
Primary and intermediate grades
Individual or group

Activity

Students are given a spelling word and a group of jumbled letters. They must find and circle the letters that appear in the correct sequence to spell the word.

Preparation

Duplicate MAKEMASTER #11 for the appropriate grade level and give one copy to each child. If you prefer, make up and duplicate a similar worksheet using words from your own spelling list or from the Chapter Word List on page 19.

Procedure

1. Have the children fold their papers back on the dotted line so that column C does not show.
2. Ask the children to say the first word in column A and then spell it aloud.
3. Then have them circle the letters in column B that appear in the correct sequence to spell the word in column A.
4. Next, tell them to turn their papers over and write the letters of the word in the correct order on the blanks in column C.
5. Have the children unfold column C to match and correct their word against the word in column A.

Variation.
Instead of having the children search for isolated letters in a group of letters to spell the word, have them find and circle the whole word as one unit within a group of letters.

MAKEMASTER 11: PRIMARY

Find the Hidden Letters

Name

A	B	C
bird	dbrxianbdria	bird
who	howoathweohwa	___
saw	awhsuwaswasom	___
club	dlabcdulbdudatb	____
their	hetiehblietiarhe	_____
first	trefrasithrtsitr	_____
tried	frtietretabidebd	_____
one	wneoaunmuwme	___
stop	tosohzptotupsou	____
form	tmfarnoferofmat	____
clam	leamcantloenpamn	____
three	fratearheatrethe	_____
sang	grosngtamunpqgu	____

MAKEMASTER 11: INTERMEDIATE

Find the Hidden Letters

Name

A	B	C
dairy	adiayrdydairyd	dairy
perform	prfeormfrorm	
expect	epxcpxetcptxe	
abroad	barboraodad	
equipment	ieuqupimpement	
fabric	arfbrabiriac	
quite	qiuietqetui	
except	ecpxpctetpt	
quiet	uiqtuiteqt	
diary	rydairyary	
aboard	aobrdorarbd	
poise	spiseopiese	
hospital	hopsiptiatlal	
several	vsaevreareal	
usually	usaulyallay	
bread	rbearderabde	

16 *Spell Well*

12

SAY IT SLOWLY
Primary or intermediate grades
Individual or group

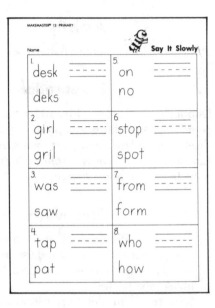

Activity

Students repeat sounds within a word in the correct sequence and then choose the correct spelling for the word.

Preparation

Duplicate MAKEMASTER #12 for the appropriate grade level and give one copy to each child. If you prefer, make up and duplicate a similar worksheet using words from your own spelling list or from the Chapter Word List on page 19. You will also need a copy of the list of words being practiced from the MAKEMASTER or worksheet.

Procedure

1. Pronounce multisyllable words (intermediate) by syllables, monosyllabic words (primary) by individual letter sounds. Then say the whole word ("sup-per, supper" or "d-e-s-k, desk").
2. Have the children repeat the sounds in the correct order and then say the whole word.
3. Ask the children to look at the spellings given on MAKEMASTER #12 for the first word.
4. Have them circle the correct spelling.
5. Write the correct word on the chalkboard and have them check and correct.
6. Finally, ask the children to write the correct spelling of the word on the line provided next to the spelling choices.

13

LISTEN AND WRITE
Primary or intermediate grades
Individual or group

Activity
Students write the correct pattern of a spoken word to practice sequencing.

Preparation
Duplicate MAKEMASTER #13 for the appropriate grade level and give one copy to each child. If you prefer, make up and duplicate a similar worksheet using words from your own spelling list or from the Chapter Word List on page 19. Words within each group should appear similar and each must be a real, not nonsense, word.

Procedure
1. Ask the children to look at the first set of words as you say each word aloud. Repeat the words and ask them to say the words along with you.
2. Say one of the four words and ask the children to copy that word on the blank next to the set.
3. Spell the word aloud or write it on the chalkboard. Have the children check and correct their responses.

Variation. Hold up a picture that corresponds to one of the words in the set instead of saying the word aloud. Have the children write that word in the blank.

MAKEMASTER 13: PRIMARY

Name _____ Listen and Write

1. grab garb grad drag	6. tires tried tied tired
2. stop step stay spot	7. cats cast calls stack
3. paste pats pals play	8. felt feel flit fell
4. grid girl grip grill	9. then three there tree
5. best bets step sets	10. name mane man none

MAKEMASTER 13: INTERMEDIATE

Name _____ Listen and Write

1. thrifty thirsty thirty	5. exception expectation exemption
2. abroad aboard abound	6. quickly quietly guilty
3. particular practical particle	7. dairy diary dreary
4. hospital hospitable hospitality	8. pious poise posies

CHAPTER ONE WORD LIST
Building Sequencing Skills for Spelling

PRIMARY

Missequence Pairs

This list contains pairs of words, each of which when missequenced, may spell the other. Above-level words which are the result of such missequencing appear in italics.

add · dad	lips · *lisp*
barn · *bran*	name · mane
best · bets	nest · nets
but · tub	nip · pin
cats · cast	now · own · won
clam · *calm*	on · no
claps · *clasp*	pat · tap
dart · *drat*	peal · leap
dog · god	sang · *snag*
eat · ate · tea	saw · was
from · form	slit · *silt*
gas · sag	snug · sung
grab · *garb*	split · *spilt*
grits · *grist*	spot · stop · pots · tops
how · who	there · three
lap · pal	tired · tried
left · felt	trap · *tarp*
lets · *lest*	trot · *tort*
lift · *flit*	

Other Commonly Missequenced Words

apple	farm	little
bird	feel	people
blue	fell	pretty
brat	first	read
card	four	shore
club	friend	their
desk	girl	third

INTERMEDIATE

Missequence Pairs

This list contains pairs of words, each of which when missequenced, may spell the other.

aboard · abroad	conserve · converse
angel · angle	corps · crops
bard · brad	crusty · curtsy
barn · bran	dairy · diary
beard · bread	except · expect
board · broad	quiet · quite
carve · crave	salve · slave
claps · clasp	spilt · split

Other Commonly Missequenced Words

about	glutton	prepare
abreast	goat	president
afraid	head	rather
animal	hospital	reason
anxious	instrument	region
babies	introduce	reindeer
brief	kite	secretary
bright	national	section
children	ornament	spaghetti
duplicate	ought	spread
exception	peaceful	storm
expectation	perform	teach
fabric	pious	their
fifth	poise	thirsty
fifty	poisonous	thirty
filter	popular	thrifty
forward	population	trunk
friend	possible	under

CHAPTER TWO

BUILDING VISUAL MEMORY SKILLS FOR SPELLING

Visual memory refers to the ability of a child to remember accurately what has been seen in the past.

There appear to be two distinct components of memory—short-term and long-term. A good speller utilizes long-term memory. He or she is able to remember over a period of time the way a whole word looks. A child needs this skill to spell well because so many of our English words are irregular or nonphonetic. Even words which are spelled as they should be pronounced pose problems when common mispronunciations have become acceptable as in *every*, pronounced *evry*.

Children who have spelling problems learn to spell words more successfully by hearing, seeing, and saying them in various combinations with repeated exposure. The activities in this chapter are basically short-term memory activities. They are intended to help the child make the transfer from revisualizing words over a short period of time to retaining the visual image over a long period of time. Then the word can more easily be recalled and spelled when needed.

In this chapter you will find activities that can be used to strengthen a child's visual memory skills. These include use of motor input such as tracing and typing, as well as use of structuring activities such as matching, focusing on shape and trouble spots, color coding, and breaking words into parts and reassembling them. In addition, we have tried to incorporate whenever possible the motor output; that is, the actual writing of the word in order to provide additional reinforcement.

14

WHAT'S MY SHAPE?
Primary grades
Individual or group

Activity
Students practice spelling words by focusing on word shapes (configurations).

Preparation
Duplicate MAKEMASTER #14 and give one copy to each child. If you prefer, make up and duplicate your own worksheet using words from your own spelling list or from the Chapter Word List on page 39.

Procedure
1. Have the children fold back the page on the dotted line so that column C cannot be seen.
2. Ask each of the children to say the first word in box 1. Then tell them to trace each letter while saying it.
3. Have them fill in the missing letters and the shape at the bottom of column A.
4. Then ask the children to look at the three shapes in column B, find the shape that matches the word in column A, and write it in.
5. Tell them to turn their papers over and write the word in the spaces provided in column C. (To increase the difficulty of the visual memory task, omit the blank spaces for each letter in column C.)
6. Then tell them to unfold their worksheets and check and correct the spelling.

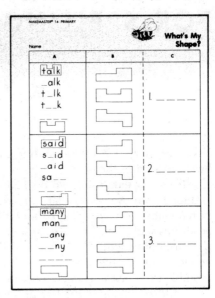

SHAPE MATCH
Primary grades
Individual or group

Activity

Students remember word configurations by matching spelling words with their shapes.

Preparation

Prepare matching pairs of cards which have the words written on one set and corresponding configurations drawn on the other set. On the backs of the configuration cards, lightly print the correct word for this configuration. You can use words from your own spelling list or from the Chapter Word List on page 39.

Procedure

1. Spread out the shape cards face up on a table and stack the word cards face down.
2. Ask one child to take the top word card, read the word, and spell it aloud.
3. Next, have this child find the corresponding configuration card on the table that matches the word card. Have the child turn over the configuration card to see if the match is correct.
4. If a correct match is made, the child then turns both cards face down, writes the word from memory, and then checks and corrects the spelling. The child keeps this pair of cards.
5. If a correct match is not made, the cards are returned to their places and the next child takes a turn.

what		what
Word card	Shape card	Back of shape card

16

MAGAZINE MATCH
Primary grades
Individual or group

Activity

Students look for words from their spelling list in magazines and newspapers in different styles of print.

Preparation

For each child you will need index cards, a copy of the child's spelling list, scissors, paste, magazines, and newspapers.

Procedure

1. Ask the children to write one spelling word from the list on each index card.
2. Have them choose one card at a time and look for that word in a magazine or newspaper. (To increase the difficulty of the visual memory task, the children can search for more than one spelling word at a time.)
3. Have them cut out the matching words they find and paste them on the index card under the word they have written.
4. Then, ask them to turn the card over and write the word.

Variation. Instead of having the children paste the matching words on the same index card, have them paste the printed words on a separate card. Have them do this for all of their words. They will then have two sets of cards. Have them shuffle all the cards together, spread them face up on the table, and match pairs. After a pair has been matched correctly, they should turn the two cards face down and write the word.

said	what	does
said	what	does

17

WATCH OUT FOR SILENT LETTERS
Primary or intermediate grades
Individual or group

Activity

Students color code (outline in a different color) the silent letters in spelling words and then write the words from memory.

Preparation

Duplicate MAKEMASTER #17 for the appropriate grade level and give one copy to each child. If you prefer, make up and duplicate a similar worksheet using words from your own spelling list or from the Chapter Word List on page 39. Give each child a colored pencil or marker.

Procedure

1. Ask the children to fold back their papers on the dotted line so that the words are facing them.
2. Tell the children to look carefully at the first word on the worksheet while you say it aloud.
3. Ask the children to repeat the word aloud and then outline the silent letter or letters with their colored markers.
4. Then have them write the whole word in the blank using regular pencils. (You might want to have them color code the silent letter or letters again for additional reinforcement.)
5. Tell them to turn the paper over and write the word.
6. Then, have them unfold the paper to check and correct.

MAKEMASTER® 17: PRIMARY

Name _____

Watch Out for Silent Letters

| 1 could |
| 2 lamb |
| 3 talk |
| 4 night |
| 5 often |
| 6 know |
| 7 sign |
| 8 high |
| 9 write |
| 10 walk |
| 11 light |
| 12 would |
| 13 bright |

MAKEMASTER® 17: INTERMEDIATE

Name _____

Watch Out for Silent Letters

| 1 tomb |
| 2 gnome |
| 3 daughter |
| 4 psalm |
| 5 climb |
| 6 height |
| 7 wrestle |
| 8 condemn |
| 9 gnat |
| 10 halves |
| 11 castle |
| 12 delight |
| 13 pneumonia |
| 14 listen |
| 15 gnaw |
| 16 through |
| 17 tongue |
| 18 balked |
| 19 knowledge |
| 20 answer |

18

CHALKBOARD TRACE
Primary grades
Individual or group

Activity

Students trace spelling words on the chalkboard with a flashlight to help them focus on individual letters in the word.

Preparation

You will need a flashlight, a spelling list, and a chalkboard. Write all the spelling words on the board in a numbered order.

Procedure

1. Make the classroom dark.
2. Have one child turn on the flashlight and find the first word.
3. Ask the child to trace each letter of the word with the flashlight as the whole group says each letter aloud as it is being traced.
4. Then ask the child to turn the flashlight off and call on another child to spell the word aloud.
5. If an error is made, have the child try the procedure again.

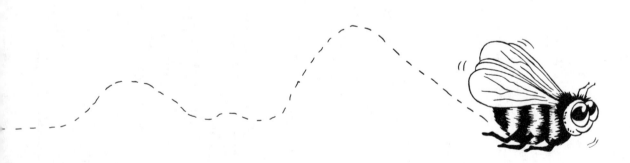

19

SPELL IT NOW
Primary or intermediate grades
Individual or group

Activity

Students briefly study a spelling word presented on a flashcard and then must revisualize the word and assemble letter or syllable cards to spell it.

Preparation

Duplicate MAKEMASTER #19 for the appropriate grade level and give one copy to each child. If you prefer, make a similar worksheet using non-phonetic words from your own spelling list or from the Chapter Word List on page 39. Then, make a set of large flashcards with one word from the MAKEMASTER on each card. Give each child a pair of scissors.

Procedure

1. Ask the children to cut apart the boxes containing either letters or syllables of the first word.
2. Tell the children to turn the letters or syllables face down and mix them up.
3. Say the first word aloud and have the children repeat it. Then hold up the flashcard for the same number of seconds as there are letters in the word.
4. Say, "Spell it now," which is the signal for the children to turn over their letters or syllables and spell the word.
5. After the children are finished, hold up the card again for them to check and correct their spelling.

Variation 1. After the last step, you can have the children turn the letters face down again and write the word from memory.

Variation 2. After the last step, you can ask the children to choose partners. Have one child turn the letters face down and spell the word aloud while the partner checks the spelling.

Variation 3. Before the children cut the words apart, you can have them color code (outline in a different color) trouble spots in the words.

MAKEMASTER 19: PRIMARY

Name _____   Spell It Now

s	a	i	d
c	o	m	e
w	a	n	t
d	o	e	s
s	o	m	e
t	h	e	y
w	e	r	e

MAKEMASTER 19: INTERMEDIATE

Name _____   Spell It Now

dif	fer	ent	
trans	por	ta	tion
fa	vor	ite	
quan	ti	ty	
ne	ces	si	ty
rea	son	a	ble
rec	og	nize	
en	vi	ron	ment
no	tor	i	ous
de	li	cious	

20 SEVEN STEPS TO SUCCESS
Intermediate grades
Individual or group

Activity

Students copy, syllabicate, and spell aloud the words while checking them against the model. Then they spell aloud and write the words without using the model.

Preparation

Duplicate MAKEMASTER #20 and give one copy to each child. Each child will also need a copy of a spelling list which has all the words written both as a whole and in syllables.

Procedure

1. Have the children copy the first word from the spelling list on the first line in the column marked *Words to Learn*.
2. Then have them say the word and make a check mark under Step 1.
3. Ask the children to write the word in syllables under Step 2.
4. Have them spell the word aloud while looking at the model, and then check Step 3.
5. Have them close their eyes and spell the word. Ask them to check the model to be sure they were correct, and then check Step 4.
6. Ask the children to write the whole word without looking at the model under Step 5. (To prevent the children from looking at the model, you may ask them to fold their papers back on the dotted line so that the model is hidden or to cover the model with an index card.)
7. Have them check and correct their spelling with the model, and then check Step 6.
8. If the children have made an error in Step 5, have them mark Step 7 and repeat all previous steps. If they have not made an error, ask them to follow the same procedure with the other words on the spelling list.

21

WHAT AM I?
Primary or intermediate grades
Individual or group

Activity

Students fill in the missing letter in a word after reading a sentence containing the word.

Preparation

Duplicate MAKEMASTER #21 for the appropriate grade level and give one copy to each child. If you prefer, make up and duplicate a similar worksheet using words from your own spelling list or from the Chapter Word List on page 39.

Procedure

1. Have the children fold back their worksheets on the dotted line and turn them over so that they see only the answers.
2. If the children are to do this activity independently, have them trace and say the words in the answer column aloud to you before they begin reading the sentences. If you do this worksheet with a group, have the children say aloud all of the words in the answer column and trace them. Point out to them the trouble spots which appear in heavier print.
3. Now have the children turn their worksheets over so that the answers are hidden and read the first sentence. When they know the missing letter or letters, have them fill in the blanks and trace all of the letters of the word.
4. Next, tell the children to unfold the worksheet, find the numbered answer which corresponds to their sentence, and check and correct it.

MAKEMASTER 21: PRIMARY

Name ___ What Am I?

Sentences	Answers
1. All of the boys go to school and then th_y go home.	4. any
2. Mary w_s playing with me last week.	6. work
3. Tommy likes to ta_k to his cat.	9. goes
4. Do you have _ny apples to eat?	7. bright
5. I think I _now how old you are.	1. they
6. He has fun doing w_rk in the yard.	3. talk
7. The bri_t sun shines all day.	2. was
8. Sam s_d he had to go home to eat.	5. know
9. Mary go_ to the pool to swim.	10. climb
10. Can you clim_ up the tree to get the cat down?	8. said

MAKEMASTER 21: INTERMEDIATE

Name ___ What Am I?

Sentences	Answers
1. The old man lit a huge cig_r.	7. ancient
2. There is more than one relig_n in the world.	10. giraffe
3. When a person has the flu, they sometimes have a bad co___.	2. religion
4. In high school, the s_ience class is one of the most important.	11. thimble
5. Does your stom___ hurt after eating too much?	1. cigar
6. Do you have tr__ble with spelling?	8. group
7. The anc__nt statue was crumbling with age.	4. science
8. To what singing gr__p do you belong?	6. trouble
9. A begg_r sat on the street with a cup in his hand.	12. machine
10. What a long-necked gira_e we saw at the zoo.	5. stomach
11. Thumbelina was as small as the size of a thimb_.	3. cough
12. The incredible ma__ine was working beautifully.	9. beggar

22 COLOR CUE
Primary or intermediate grades
Individual or group

Activity

Students color code the trouble spots in spelling words and rewrite each word from memory.

Preparation

Duplicate MAKEMASTER #22 for the appropriate grade level and give one copy to each child. If you prefer, make up and duplicate a similar worksheet using words from your own spelling list or from the Chapter Word List on page 39. Each child will need a brightly colored marker.

Procedure

1. Ask the children to fold their papers on the dotted line.
2. Ask the children to outline with their colored markers the underlined letters in the words listed.
3. Next have them say the first word and then trace over the letters with the index finger of their writing hand, saying each letter aloud as it is traced.
4. Tell them to trace the word several times with their pencils.
5. Then have them write the word in the blank space provided.
6. They should next turn their papers over and write the word from memory in the column that has been folded over.
7. Have them unfold their papers and check and correct their answers.

MAKEMASTER 22: PRIMARY

Name _____   Color Clue

Trace	Write		Write
1. worm	_____	1.	_____
2. would	_____	2.	_____
3. two	_____	3.	_____
4. does	_____	4.	_____
5. want	_____	5.	_____
6. other	_____	6.	_____
7. believe	_____	7.	_____
8. color	_____	8.	_____
9. little	_____	9.	_____
10. their	_____	10.	_____
11. white	_____	11.	_____
12. watch	_____	12.	_____
13. very	_____	13.	_____

MAKEMASTER 22: INTERMEDIATE

Name _____   Color Clue

Trace	Write		Write
1. build	_____	1.	_____
2. women	_____	2.	_____
3. poison	_____	3.	_____
4. young	_____	4.	_____
5. bicycle	_____	5.	_____
6. museum	_____	6.	_____
7. because	_____	7.	_____
8. bargain	_____	8.	_____
9. recognize	_____	9.	_____
10. guard	_____	10.	_____
11. eager	_____	11.	_____
12. toward	_____	12.	_____
13. cousin	_____	13.	_____
14. bracelet	_____	14.	_____

23

REMEMBER IT
Primary or intermediate grades
Individual or group

Activity

Students look at spelling words on a chart and write them after a time lapse in order to strengthen long-term memory.

Preparation

Devise and duplicate a spelling list from the Chapter Word List on page 39. Make a corresponding wall chart with these words. Tape the chart to the wall at the back of the room. Provide each child with a copy of the spelling list, paper, and pencil.

Procedure

1. Have the children walk to the back of the room to look at the wall chart.
2. Have them look at the first word and spell it aloud.
3. Then have them return to their desks and write the word on their papers.
4. Next, tell them to check and correct their spellings, using their personal copies of the spelling list.
5. If the children have misspelled the word, have them repeat the procedure until they spell the word correctly.

Variation. You may have the children follow the above procedure but have them work in pairs. One partner should check the answers of the other.

24 MISSING LETTER BINGO
Primary or intermediate grades
Individual or group

Activity

Students fill in the missing letters in words as they are dictated and mark each one called. To win they must have four words in a row marked and they must spell correctly all four words.

Preparation

For each child, you will need a large sheet of paper, such as newsprint, and markers, such as clips or index cards. Each child will also need a spelling list which has been written so that each word has a blank space where one letter has been omitted. If you prefer, you may write this spelling list on the chalkboard for the group.

Procedure

1. Have the children divide their large sheets of paper into 16 parts by folding them.
2. Ask them to write one word from the spelling list in each space (words should be written in random order), leaving out a letter as has been done on the list.
3. Say a spelling word from the list and have the children find the word on their papers.
4. Ask them to fill in the missing letter and cover the word with a marker.
5. Have the children proceed as in Bingo. The winner must spell the words in the completed Bingo in order to win the game.

Variation 1. You may individualize this activity by determining the area of difficulty of each word for the child. Then color code the trouble spot for the child on his or her spelling list. The color coded letter(s) becomes the letter(s) the child omits when making the playing board.

Variation 2. After the children have finished making their playing boards, you may collect and redistribute them so that each child plays from a paper written by a classmate.

Variation 3. After the Bingo game is completed, you may recycle the playing boards by having the children fill in the missing letters of the remaining words. Then have them cut the boards into 16 boxes with one word on each. Two children can then combine their cards to play Concentration. (See Activity 27, *What a Pair*, page 39.)

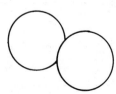

25 ERASURE GAME
Primary or intermediate grades
Individual or group

Activity
Students view and memorize several spelling words written on the chalkboard. Then they close their eyes and one word is erased. They must recall and write the missing word.

Preparation
You will need a chalkboard, chalk, eraser, and a spelling list.

Procedure
1. Write three or four spelling words from the list on the chalkboard.
2. Ask the children to look at the words and memorize the spellings.
3. Have the children close their eyes while you erase one of the words.
4. Then tell them to look at the remaining words and write on their papers the word which was erased from the board.
5. Call on a child to spell the word aloud. After the child spells it correctly, have the child write the word on the chalkboard.
6. Repeat this procedure, erasing a different word each time. Continue with three or four other words from the spelling list.

Variation. You can have the children play this as a game, working in pairs. Have one child write the words and erase one word while the other one spells the erased word.

◄ Board for Missing Letter Bingo

run_ing	fun_y	sad_y	bit_en
hop_ing	g◯h	ste_ping	flip_ing
j◯d	mad_er	sai_or	mop_ed
sad_ess	turn_r	stop_ed	p◯

26 BACK TRACE
Primary or intermediate grades
Individual or group

Activity

Students trace words on one another's backs, and then rewrite the words on paper.

Preparation

Prepare a list of spelling words from your own spelling list or from the Chapter Word List on page 39 to distribute to each child. Have the children work in pairs.

Procedure

1. Ask one child from each pair to trace the letters of one of the spelling words on the partner's back, saying each letter as it is traced.
2. Then have the tracer say the whole word aloud.
3. Next, tell both children to write the word from memory, check, and correct before going on to the next word.
4. When the tracer has gone through these steps with all of the words on the list, then have the partners reverse roles.

Variation.
To increase the difficulty of this activity, you can have one child trace the letters without saying them while the other child says the letter names and then says the whole word. Then have them both write the word as in the above procedure.

27

WHAT A PAIR
Primary or intermediate grades
Individual or group

Activity

Students memorize spelling words by playing a Concentration card game which requires that children visually recall words and their position in a group of word cards.

Preparation

Copy each word from a spelling list onto two index cards of uniform size. Use words from your own spelling list or from the Chapter Word List on page 39.

Procedure

1. Shuffle the cards and place them face down on the table.
2. Ask the first child to turn over two cards and say each word aloud.
3. If the cards match, have the child take the cards and turn them face down. The child then spells the word from memory.
4. If the word is spelled correctly, the child keeps the cards and takes another turn.
5. If the two cards turned over do not match or if the child does not spell the word correctly, then ask the child to show the cards to all of the other players and then put the cards back in their original places, face down on the table.

Variation 1. For primary grade children, you can make cards with pictures of the words next to them.

Variation 2. You can make matching cards featuring troublesome letters with similar configurations, such as *b*, *p*, and *d*. Make sure that you draw a line in another color at the bottom of each card.

28

PROGRAMMED SPELLING PRACTICE
Intermediate grades
Individual or group

Activity

Students focus on the correct spelling of individual syllables as a way of memorizing the spelling of a whole word.

Preparation

Duplicate MAKEMASTER #28 and give one copy to each child. Prepare a mask (a card or a piece of paper) for each child to cover answers on the MAKEMASTER sheet.

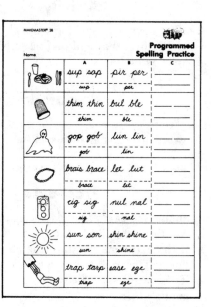

Procedure

1. Have the children place the mask under the horizontal dotted line below the first row of syllables, covering the answers.
2. Have the children look at the picture in the first row and say the word aloud.
3. Ask them to look at column A and underline the first syllable in the pictured word.
4. Ask them to underline the second syllable in the word in column B.
5. Have them move the mask down to the next dotted line and check their answers. If there are errors, have the children correct them.
6. Have them fold over column C so that columns A and B are face down. Ask them to write the word divided into syllables on the first line in column C and then write the whole word on the next line.

29 BREAK IT UP

Intermediate grades
Individual or group

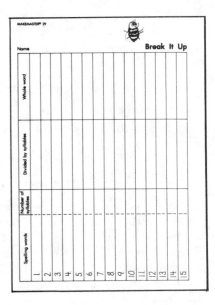

Activity

Students divide multisyllabic words into separate syllables and then write the word without looking at the model.

Preparation

Duplicate MAKEMASTER #29 and give one copy to each child. Each child should also have a copy of the spelling list.

Procedure

1. Have the children write the words from the spelling list in the numbered column of MAKEMASTER #29.
2. Ask the children to look at the first word in this column and say the word by syllables.
3. Have them count the number of syllables in the word and write that number in the column called *Number of Syllables*.
4. Then have them fold back the numbered column so that the model is hidden.
5. Ask them to write the word by syllables into the column called *Divided by Syllables*. Tell them to look at the model, check, and correct.
6. Have them write the word correctly in the column called *Whole Word*.

30

TYPE IT OUT
Primary or intermediate grades
Individual or group

Activity

Students type rows of words from their spelling list.

Preparation

Duplicate MAKEMASTER #30 for the appropriate grade level and give one copy to each child. Each child will need a typewriter, a piece of paper, and a pencil.

Procedure

1. Have the children type the first word on the typing form on MAKE-MASTER #30 directly to the right of the word.
2. Ask them to check and correct the word they have typed against the model and retype it if necessary.
3. Have them type the word again and check again to be sure it is correct. Have them continue typing the word across the page.
4. When the children have finished typing a row of the word, have them write it on a piece of paper. Be sure that they check and correct before going on to the next word.
5. When the children have finished typing all of the words, have them remove the paper from the typewriter and proofread by crossing out all incorrect spellings.

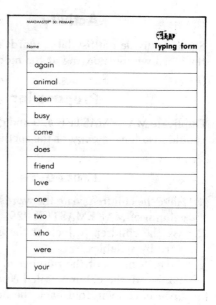

MAKEMASTER® 30: PRIMARY

Name _____ Typing form

| again |
| animal |
| been |
| busy |
| come |
| does |
| friend |
| love |
| one |
| two |
| who |
| were |
| your |

MAKEMASTER® 30: INTERMEDIATE

Name _____ Typing form

| acre |
| anxious |
| athlete |
| bicycle |
| colonel |
| guard |
| knife |
| language |
| onion |
| picnic |
| precious |
| rhythm |
| sugar |
| toward |
| twelve |
| villain |
| woman |
| young |

CHAPTER TWO WORD LIST
Building Visual Memory Skills for Spelling

PRIMARY

Nonphonetic Spellings

above	father	shirt
again	four	should
air	friend	some
animal	fur	son
any	give	sun
apple	goes	sure
are	have	the
balloon	hear	their
beauty	here	there
become	key	they
been	kitchen	to
believe	learn	true
blue	little	turn
board	live	two
bread	love	very
brother	many	want
burn	money	was
bush	more	watch
busy	mother	water
buy	move	were
carry	of	where
circus	oh	while
city	once	white
color	one	who
come	other	why
could	people	word
dear	please	work
do	pretty	world
does	put	worm
done	ready	would
ear	really	year
earn	said	you
eyes	saw	your

Silent Letters

bright	knit	often
chalk	knob	right
climb	knock	sign
comb	lamb	talk
high	light	walk
knee	might	write
knew	night	

INTERMEDIATE

Nonphonetic Spellings

acre
against
ancient
anxious
apron
aunt
bargain
barrel
beautiful
because
beggar
bicycle
bracelet
breakfast
build
cedar
cellar
cigar
colonel
course
cousin
decide
delicious
diamond
dollar

eager
enough
favorite
field
fruit
gasoline
giraffe
group
guard
guess
juice
language
mosquito
museum
necessity
neighbor
notorious
ocean
octave
onion
orchard
peculiar
period
picnic
piece

poison
precious
prove
quantity
reasonable
recognize
religion
rhythm
soldier
someone
sugar
suit
sunshine
supper
thimble
toward
transportation
trapeze
view
villain
whisper
woman
women
young
yourself

Silent Letters

aisle
answer
assignment
autumn
bought
business
caught
christen
clothes
column
cupboard
daughter
deign
designer
eight
exhibit
fasten
folk
foreign
ghost

gnarled
gnaw
gnome
half
hasten
hymn
island
knelt
knife
knight
knockout
knot
knowledge
limb
listen
naughty
psalm
psychology
salmon
scenery

science
scissors
sleigh
straight
taught
though
thought
through
tomb
tonight
trouble
unknown
weigh
weight
Wednesday
whistle
wouldn't
wrestle
wrote
yolk

PRIMARY AND INTERMEDIATE

Alternate Sounds for Letters

absence
acre
architect
character
cough
elephant

enough
laugh
machine
nephew
orchid
physical

physician
schedule
school
stomach
telephone

CHAPTER THREE

BUILDING POSITION-IN-SPACE RECOGNITION SKILLS FOR SPELLING

The term *position-in-space* recognition refers to the ability to perceive the position of a letter in relation to the observer's orientation in space. For example, *b* must be written correctly in space or it will appear as *d*, *p*, *q*, *g*, or *9*.

Position-in-space difficulties are seen in children's spelling when, for instance, the child spells *bog* for *dog* or *np* for *up*. This same child will have difficulty distinguishing in which direction the letters are turned. Many times these difficulties indicate that a child has not learned to distinguish right from left or top from bottom.

Position-in-space problems have a high correlation to inadequate visual memory. Obviously, if a child has a poor visual memory, then position-in-space recognition is affected since the child cannot remember in which directions the distinguishing parts of letters are to go.

The activities in this chapter are geared to give the child with position-in-space difficulties practice in recognizing and writing those letters and words which are most easily confused. Children should practice tracing tactile letters made by using felt, sandpaper, glitter, sand, salt, or hardened glue. It is further suggested that a chart with the letters of the alphabet be in full view of the children at all times so that they will always have a correct model to copy. If children are making persistent errors with position-in-space of certain letters, it might be helpful to give them an individual card with the trouble letters written on it to attach to their desks.

31

PAINT THE CHALKBOARD
Primary grades
Individual or group

Activity

Students write troublesome letters or words first with a water-soaked paint-brush on the board and then with a pencil on paper.

Preparation

You will need a large paintbrush, a can of water, and a chalkboard. Also have a list of troublesome letters or words such as those included in the Chapter Word List on page 51. Each child will need a pencil and paper.

Procedure

1. Write the first letter or word from the list on the chalkboard.
2. Ask the child to "paint" a row of letters or words next to the one you have written on the board with the wet paintbrush. Ask the child to use large strokes when making each letter and to say the name of the letter or pronounce the word as it is being written.
3. Tell the child to check each letter with the model before continuing to the next one.
4. Next ask the child to write this letter or word in a row several times on a piece of paper.
5. Ask the child to return to the chalkboard with the paper to check and correct.

32 STICK 'EM UP!
Primary grades
Individual or group

Activity

Students choose from a set of cards the correct letter that matches the letter dictated by the instructor.

Preparation

Make a set of cards for each child, using trouble letters such as those included in the Chapter Word List on page 51. Print the letter on both sides of the card, placing a line at the bottom. Use an opaque paper or card stock so that when the card is held up, the letters do not show through. Each child will also need a pencil and paper. You will need a set of large letter cards and several cards which feature words containing these letters for yourself.

Child's cards

Procedure

1. Have the children place their sets of letter cards in a row with the bottom line of each card nearest to them.
2. Say the letter on the first of your letter cards and have the children find their letter card that matches this letter.
3. Then say, "Stick 'Em Up!" which is the signal for the children to hold up the card they have chosen.
4. Then show your card to the children and have them match their cards with yours. Then tell them to write that letter on their papers.
5. If one of them has held up an incorrect card, give that child a chance to change the card until a correct match has been made.

Variation. Once the children can correctly identify single letters, dictate words and have them hold up the letter with which that word begins. Then have them write this word on their papers, copying it from your card if necessary.

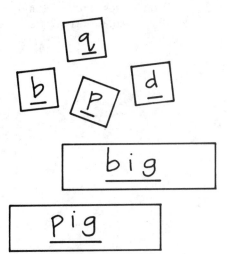

Teacher's cards

33

FIND THE ODD BALL
Primary grades
Individual or group

Activity

Students trace letters or words within a group and identify which letter or word is different from the rest.

Preparation

Duplicate MAKEMASTER #33 and distribute one copy to each child. If you prefer, make a worksheet using trouble letters or words such as the ones included in the Chapter Word List on page 51.

Procedure

1. Ask the children to trace each letter or word in the row saying its name or sound, or pronouncing the word at the same time.
2. Ask them to cross out the letter or word that is not the same as the others.
3. Next have them write the letter or word in the space provided at the end of the row.

MAKEMASTER 33

Name _____   Find the Odd Ball

1. b b b b d b b b b b b b b b b
2. n n n n n n n u n n n n n n
3. z z z z z z z z z z s z z z z
4. g g g g q g g g g g g g g g
5. s s s s s s s e s s s s s s s s
6. d d d d p d d d d d d d d d
7. big big dig big big big
8. mad map mad mad
9. saw saw saw eaw saw
10. gun gun qun gun gun
11. beak peak beak beak

34 COUNT IT UP
Primary grades
Group

Activity

Students identify a troublesome letter after listening to its name or a word in which it is contained. Then, they find it in a row among letters whose position-in-space is easily confused.

Preparation

Duplicate MAKEMASTER #34 and distribute one sheet to each child, or make a similar worksheet using letters or words from the Chapter Word List on page 51. The children will need small blank cards and a pencil.

Procedure

1. Tell the children to look at one row as you say a letter or word. Have them circle and trace the letter or word they heard every time it appears in that row.
2. Have them write the letter or word practiced in the space at the end of each row.
3. Then have them write on a card the number of letters or words they circled and hold up the card as a means of checking the correct answer with you.

35

TV TRAY PLAY
Primary grades
Individual

Activity

Students trace a word they read on a card, etch the word into clay, and then rewrite the word on paper.

Preparation

Make up a spelling list containing words such as those included in the Chapter Word List on page 51. Write each word on a card. Provide an aluminum or styrofoam tray (such as a frozen dinner container) and some clay which should be pounded flat to cover the bottom of the tray. The child will also need a piece of paper and two pencils, one for writing in clay and one for writing on paper.

Procedure

1. Have the child take the first card and read the word.
2. Have the child trace the word, saying each letter aloud.
3. Next, tell the child to write the word in clay with a pencil, again saying each letter aloud.
4. Tell the child to check and correct the word against the word on the card.
5. Next have the child turn the card over and "erase" the word written in the clay.
6. Now ask the child to write the word on paper. Have the child check and correct by turning over the card.

36

TRACE YOUR STEPS
Primary or intermediate grades
Group

Activity

Students find letters and words in a row that match the first one presented to them, and then rewrite that letter or word.

Preparation

Duplicate MAKEMASTER #36 for the appropriate grade level and distribute one to each child. If you make your own worksheet, be sure that you begin each row of choices with the correct letter or word for reinforcement.

Procedure

1. Ask the children to trace the first letter or word with a pencil. (Make sure that primary grade children begin the stroke for each letter where the arrow on the MAKEMASTER indicates.) You might also ask the children to say the sound or name of the letter, or pronounce the word.
2. Then have the children find and trace each of the letters or words which matches the first one in the row. At the same time have them say the letter sound or name, or pronounce the word again.
3. Tell the children to write that letter or word in the space provided at the end of each row.

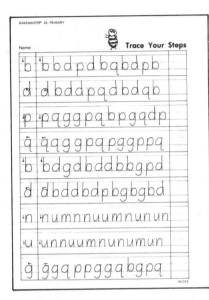

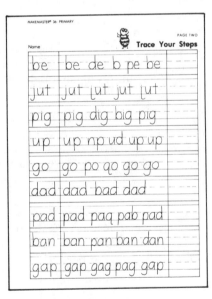

37

PICK THE POCKET
Primary or intermediate grades
Individual or group

Activity

Students use a pocket chart to play a letter or word identification game.

Preparation

Make a pocket chart, letter or word cards, and markers as shown in the il-lustration. Make one marker to correspond with each space on the chart and place them in a pile. Each child will need a piece of paper and a pencil.

Procedure

1. Ask a child to choose a marker from the pile.
2. Have the child go to the chart and read the letter or word the marker indicates.
3. If it is read correctly, tell the child to keep the card and discard the marker.
4. Then ask all the children to write that letter or spell that word on their paper.
5. Have them check their answers by having the child with that card stand and show it to the group.
6. If a card is read incorrectly, ask the child to leave the card on the chart, and retrieve and return the marker to the pile.
7. Ask another child to pick a marker and follow the same procedure. Continue in this manner until all the markers are gone.

Variation 1. As a follow-up activity, ask one child to choose a tag and read it to another child. Have that child locate the cor-rect letter card and read it aloud while the first child writes it on the chalk-board. If the first child writes the letters correctly, let that child keep the card.

Variation 2. If you want to apply this activity to building visual memory skills, use the above procedure with prefixes, suffixes, or words from the Chapter Word List for Building Visual Memory Skills for Spelling on page 51.

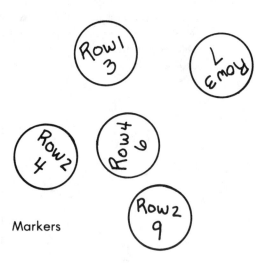

Markers

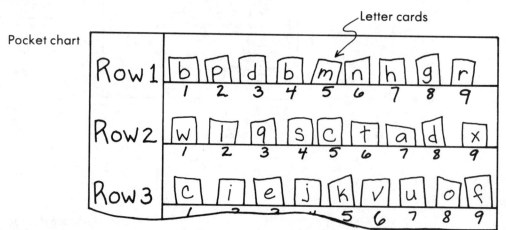

Letter cards

Pocket chart

38 DOMINOES
Primary or intermediate grades
Group

Activity
Students play the game of dominoes, matching letters or words.

Preparation
Make a set of "dominoes" with matching letters or words rather than dots. Pass out the same number of dominoes to each child. Make sure there are some extras for the draw pile. Several children may play this game together.

Procedure
1. The first child to begin is the one who can place a double (same letter or word on both sides of the domino) on the table.
2. Ask the children to write down each word they use after their turn and check their answer by matching it with the domino.
3. Ask the next player to find a domino with a letter or word that matches one already placed on the table and place it next to this domino.
4. If this player cannot find a match, then have this child take a new domino from the draw pile until a match is made.
5. The game is over when one player has no more dominoes left.

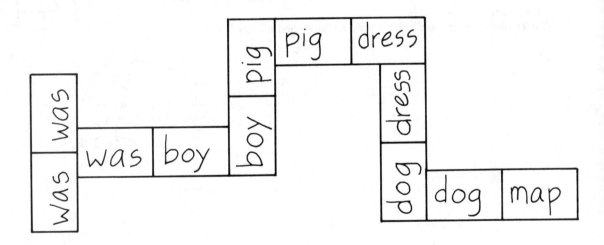

39

GO FISH

Primary or intermediate grades
Group

Activity

Students play a card game which involves matching letters or words.

Preparation

Make matching cards in the same color paper containing letters or words from the Chapter Word List on page 51. (For example, two blue *bs*, two red *ps*, and so on.) Make sure the bottom of each card is marked with a line to distinguish the top from the bottom. Pass out the same number of cards to each player and put the extras in the "fish" pile. Each child will need a piece of paper and pencil.

Procedure

1. Ask the first child to begin by placing all matching pairs he or she already holds on the table.
2. Have the child write this letter or word on a piece of paper.
3. The same child then asks another player for a card needed to make another pair.
4. If the player has the needed card, it is given to the first child. If this player does not have the card, the first child is instructed to "Go fish."
5. Then the child must take a card from the "fish" pile and the next child takes a turn.
6. The game continues until one player has matched all cards held.

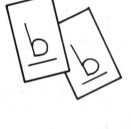

CHAPTER THREE WORD LIST
Building Position-in-Space Recognition Skills for Spelling

PRIMARY
Words That Are Confused

bad · dad · dab	fuss · fuzz
bat · pat	gun · gut
bay · day	jam · jaw
beak · peak	joke · yoke
bed · beg	jut · put
big · dig · pig	lad · lap
box · boy	mad · map
buck · duck	mall · wall
cab · cap	met · wet
die · pie	mill · will
dine · pine	pet · get
dress · press	pit · quit
dry · pry	sip · zip

Words That Feature Trouble Letters

body	dead	run
close	guess	up

INTERMEDIATE
Words That Are Confused

babble · dabble	gaunt · jaunt
bare · dare	guilt · quilt
buck · duck	pick · quick
garden · pardon	

Words That Feature Trouble Letters

adept	doubt	plaid
broad	edible	queen
bridge	gnome	suit
bugle	guide	wiggle
debt	guilty	
double	money	

PRIMARY AND INTERMEDIATE
Trouble Letters

b	m	u
d	n	w
f	p	y
g	q	z
j	s	

CHAPTER FOUR

BUILDING VISUAL DISCRIMINATION SKILLS FOR SPELLING

Visual discrimination refers to the ability to differentiate the visual form of one letter from another. In order to spell words correctly, children must be able to see fine differences between similar letters and words.

Children who are experiencing difficulty with visual discrimination are confused by letters or words with similar configurations. They have difficulty seeing the difference between *m* and *n*, *h* and *n*, *j* and *g*, and so on; and between words written in cursive such as *feel* and *fell* and *puff* and *pull*. These children must learn the unique features that distinguish similar letters and words.

The activities in this chapter are designed to give children practice in spelling words which contain letters that are visually similar and words which have configurations that might be confused. If children continue to make errors in visual discrimination, it might be helpful to have them verbalize the differences that they see between letters (for example, "*m* has two humps and *n* has one").

40

MATCHMAKERS
Primary grades
Individual or group

Activity

Students match pairs of words, then rewrite them from memory.

Preparation

Duplicate MAKEMASTER #40 and give one copy to each child, or make a worksheet using words from the Chapter Word List on page 59. Each box on the worksheet must be large enough to be cut into four pieces by the children (with one word in each section). Each child will also need a pair of scissors, a piece of paper, and a pencil.

Procedure

1. Have the children read aloud the words in the boxes on the worksheet. Be sure they read all of the words in each box before going to the next box.
2. Ask them to trace over the letters of each word while saying each letter aloud.
3. Then have them cut out all the boxes on the heavy lines. Next have them cut each box into four pieces on the dotted lines that separate the words.
4. Ask them to mix up the words and match the pairs.
5. When all pairs have been matched, have the children turn one pair of words face down and write that word on their papers. Have them write each word pair on their papers and check and correct each one by turning over the pairs.

Variation. These word boxes may be used by the children to play *What a Pair*, Concentration game (see Activity 27 on page 35).

MAKEMASTER 40

Name _____

Matchmakers

feel	fell	map	nap
feel	fell	map	nap
ran	ram	girl	grill
ran	ram	girl	grill
jog	joy	fill	till
jog	joy	fill	till
cat	oat	bat	hat
cat	oat	bat	hat

41

FINGER FUN
Primary grades
Individual or group

Activity

Students trace troublesome letters (alone and within words) and write them to reinforce the correct visual form of the letters.

Preparation

You will need to make two cards for each letter you want the children to practice. One card of each pair will have the troublesome letter on it, which has been embossed with felt, sandpaper, glue, or salt (see introduction to *Building Position-in-Space Recognition Skills for Spelling* on page 41). The other card will have a complete word containing that letter, with the troublesome letter boldly embossed. Each child will need a set of cards, a piece of paper, and a pencil.

Procedure

1. Ask the children to take the first pair of cards, say the name of the letter, and read the word aloud.
2. Next, have them trace the individual letter and then trace the word, saying each letter as it is traced.
3. Then instruct the children to turn their letter and word pair over and write the word on their papers from memory.
4. Finally, they should turn the cards over to check and correct.

Variation. To make this activity more difficult, you can give the children two word cards for each letter card and have them choose the one that goes with the letter card. For example, for *n* you could give *ran* and *ram*.

42

MATCH AND SEE
Primary or intermediate grades
Individual or group

Activity

Students match and trace the correct letter or word from a row of letters or words to see fine differences in letter form.

Preparation

Duplicate MAKEMASTER #42 for the appropriate grade level and give one copy to each child. If you prefer, make up and duplicate a similar worksheet using words from your own spelling list or from the Chapter Word List on page 59.

Procedure

1. Have the children fold their papers back on the dotted line.
2. Ask the children to say the letter or word in the left-hand column.
3. Have them trace the letter or word with their pencils, saying each letter aloud as it is traced.
4. Ask them to find and trace each of the letters or words which matches the one in the left-hand column.
5. Have them turn their papers over and write the letter or word in the blank column.

MAKEMASTER 42: PRIMARY

Name _____ Match and See

a	aodaadbaoad	-----
i	ijliijjiililjiilj	-----
h	hbnhhbnhhnb	-----
y	yggyypyghygy	-----
v	vwmvwwvwmvv	-----
f	fttfftftfffttf	-----
it	if if it if it it ti if	-----
ran	ram ran ran ram rau	-----
vine	vine wine wine viue	-----
oat	oat cat aot cat oat	-----
fan	tan fan fan fun tan	-----
puff	putt puff put puff	-----

MAKEMASTER 42: INTERMEDIATE

Name _____ Match and See

m	m m n w m m m n m	
f	l l f t f f b j l b f f l f	
e	e e l e i e e l e e i l e e	
u	u w u u v v u w u u n	
t	t f r j t b f i t f f f i t	
l	l e f f l l e l e f l l e l	
chimp	chimp chinp chimp chimp	
joined	joined foined joimed joined	
feeler	feller feeler feeler feleer	
loose	loose lose lose loose	
every	every ever very every	
attack	attach attack attach attack	
simple	simple single simple simple	
thirty	thrifty thirty thrifty thirty	
filth	filth fifeh filth fifeh	
angle	angel angle angle angel	
chose	choose chose chose choose	
curtain	certain curtain curtain certain	
odor	odor order odor order	
insisted	insisted instead insisted	
even	ever evem even wen ever	
hotel	hostel hotel hostel hotel	
mummy	mummy munny mummy mummy	
pebble	pebble peffle pebbel pebble	

43

LOOK CAREFULLY
Primary or intermediate grades
Individual or group

Activity

Students discriminate between two similarly spelled words and choose the word that is correct within the context of a sentence.

Preparation

Duplicate MAKEMASTER #43 for the appropriate grade level and give one copy to each child. If you prefer, make up and duplicate a similar worksheet using words from your own spelling list or from the Chapter Word List on page 59. Each child will also need a pencil.

Procedure

1. Have the children trace over the word in A with their pencils saying each letter aloud as it is traced.
2. Have them look at B, read the sentence, and circle the correct word to complete the sentence.
3. Tell them to write the correct word on the blank in C.

MAKEMASTER® 43: PRIMARY

Name   Look Carefully

1. A. nut
   B. The squirrel ate a large nut/hut
   C. The squirrel ate a large____
2. A. run
   B. I like to rum/run very fast.
   C. I like to ____very fast.
3. A. tan
   B. You can get a good tan/fan at the beach.
   C. You can get a good____ at the beach.
4. A. boy
   B. Go and ask that bog/boy to help you.
   C. Go and ask that____ to help you.
5. A. feel
   B. A warm bath will fell/feel good.
   C. A warm bath will ____ good.

MAKEMASTER® 43: INTERMEDIATE

Name   Look Carefully

1. A. ankle
   B. The athlete sprained his angle/ankle.
   C. The athlete sprained his ____.
2. A. chose
   B. He choose/chose five members for the team.
   C. He ____ five members for the team.
3. A. odor
   B. The blossoms have a pleasant odor/order.
   C. The blossoms have a pleasant ____.
4. A. attach
   B. We will attack/attach the strings to the kites.
   C. We will ____ the strings to the kites.
5. A. certain
   B. Are you certain/curtain that is the man you saw?
   C. Are you ____ that is the man you saw?
6. A. thrifty
   B. It pays to be a thirty/thrifty shopper.
   C. It pays to be a ____ shopper.
7. A. every
   B. He always completes every/even homework assignment.
   C. He always completes ____ homework assignment.
8. A. farther
   B. Mr. Smith must travel father/farther than Dad.
   C. Mr. Smith must travel ____ than Dad.
9. A. instead
   B. She asked for fried potatoes instead/insisted of mashed.
   C. She asked for fried potatoes ____ of mashed.

44

LOOK ALIKES
Primary or intermediate grades
Individual or group

Activity

Students find and trace two identical words in a row of words which appear similar and then write the word.

Preparation

Duplicate MAKEMASTER #44 for the appropriate grade level and give one copy to each child. If you prefer, make up and duplicate a similar worksheet using words from your own spelling list or from the Chapter Word List on page 59. Each child will need a pencil.

Procedure

1. Have the children look carefully at the words in the first row and find the two words which are exactly the same.
2. Then, have them trace over the two words they have located, saying each letter aloud as it is traced.
3. Finally, ask them to write the word in the blank space at the end of the row.

MAKEMASTER 44: PRIMARY

Name _____ Look Alikes

1. cot cat cof caf col cat _____
2. fan tam fon tan fam fan _____
3. bat bof baf hat hat bal _____
4. silt sift sitt sift siff _____
5. aat cat act oat aot oat _____
6. name nane nome name mane _____
7. ever even ewer euer even _____
8. noom none noon nome noon _____
9. vet wet wef wet vef wel _____
10. feet fell feel fell feef _____
11. happy bappy baggy happy _____
12. nome home hone home none _____

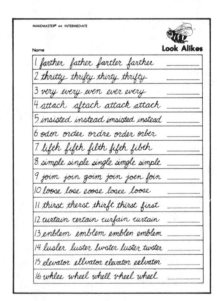

MAKEMASTER 44: INTERMEDIATE

Name _____ Look Alikes

1. farther father fartler farther _____
2. thritty thrifty thirty thrifty _____
3. very every even ever every _____
4. attach aftach attack attach _____
5. insisted instead imsisted instead _____
6. odor ordee ordre order orber _____
7. lifth fifth filth fifth fibth _____
8. simple sinple single simple simple _____
9. joim join goim join joen foin _____
10. loose lose eoose losee loose _____
11. thirst therst thirft thirst first _____
12. curtain certain curfain curtain _____
13. enblem emblem emblen emblem _____
14. lusler luster lwster luster twster _____
15. elevator ellvator elevator eelvator _____
16. whlee wheel whell vheel wheel _____

CHAPTER FOUR WORD LIST
Building Visual Discrimination Skills for Spelling

PRIMARY

Words That Have Similar Configurations

bat · hat
bog · boy
cat · cot · oat
fan · tan
feel · fell
fill · till
hat · hot
hut · nut

if · it
jog · joy
map · nap
puff · pull
ran · ram
run · rum
wine · vine

Trouble Letters That Have Similar Configurations

a · c · o
b · h · n
f · t

g · p · y
i · j

m · n · r
u · v · w

INTERMEDIATE

Words That Have Similar Configurations

angle · ankle
attach · attack
certain · curtain
choose · chose
cover · cower
even · ever
every · very

farther · father
fifth · filth
hostel · hotel
jabber · gabber
jello · yellow
loose · lose
simple · single

Trouble Letters That Have Similar Configurations

a · o
b · l
e · i · l
f · g

g · j · q
h · k
m · n
n · r

u · v · w
y · z

CHAPTER FIVE

BUILDING AUDITORY DISCRIMINATION SKILLS FOR SPELLING

Auditory discrimination refers to the ability to hear similarities and differences between sounds within a word. Children who are having difficulty with auditory discrimination may be hearing parts of a word selectively and, therefore, leaving out sounds or word parts when they spell the word (such as *rember* for *remember*). Another type of error these children may make occurs when they hear parts of a word incorrectly and, consequently, write the word the way it was heard (*inter* for *enter*, or *chain* for *train*).

Many auditory discrimination errors are compounded when children fail to hear a sound within a word or hear sounds incorrectly and, consequently, *mispronounce* that word. The mispronounced word is then likely to be spelled the way it is said (*libary* for *library*, or *suprise* for *surprise*). For that reason, in each activity in this chapter the teacher pronounces and the children repeat all of the words used in that activity. It is especially important for you to be sure the children are pronouncing words correctly before they proceed to the rest of each activity.

Dialectical speech may make it appear that a child is having auditory discrimination difficulty when, in fact, the situation is really one of pronunciation differences (*idear* for *idea*, or *warsh* for *wash*). It is important to analyze the types of errors the children are making to assess whether there is a problem with actually hearing sounds correctly.

It often appears that children who are making errors in auditory discrimination have not learned to auditorize (say the word to themselves) as a way of monitoring what they have spelled after having written it. Auditorizing is important because it helps children to remember to include all word sounds and syllables pronounced, and to correct themselves if a sound has been left out of the spelling. As you assist the children with activities in this chapter, you may want to encourage them to monitor their own work by teaching them this important step.

Note that the activities in this section can be taped for individual or small group use so that the children can work independently.

45

CLOSE THE GAP
Primary or intermediate grades
Individual or group

Activity

Students choose the correct letter or letter combination to fill in the missing sound which will complete a dictated word.

Preparation

Duplicate MAKEMASTER #45 for the appropriate grade level and give one copy to each child. If you prefer, make up and duplicate a similar worksheet using words from your own spelling list or from the Chapter Word List on page 68. You will also need a list of the spelling words on the MAKEMASTER or worksheet.

Procedure

1. Have the children fold their papers back on the dotted line.
2. Say the first word on your list aloud and ask the children to repeat it.
3. Have them look at the choices to the right of the word and trace the letter or letter combination that would complete the first word.
4. Then ask them the sound that the letter or letters make in that word.
5. Tell them to write the missing letter(s) in the blank(s) in the word and say the word aloud.
6. Then have them turn their papers over and write the word in the blank column.
7. Have them unfold their papers to check and correct before you continue with the next word.

Variation 1. Use nonsense words instead of real words so that children rely on auditory discrimination, not visual memory, to transcribe the words.

Variation 2. Offer three similar real words as choices (*spit*, *spat*, *spot*) and dictate a different word each time.

MAKEMASTER 45: PRIMARY

Name _____ Close the Gap

1	sp_t	i, a, o
2	fle___	sh, ch
3	p_n	i, a, e
4	to___	t, b, p
5	_ck	i, e, u
6	hun___	ch, sh
7	_ace	f, th, v
8	ca___	p, t, b
9	w_nt	i, e, u
10	__at	th, f, v
11	_oll___	d, th, t
12	__ain	tr, ch
13	__ink	dr, tr
14	p_t	e, i, o

MAKEMASTER 45: INTERMEDIATE

Name _____ Close the Gap

1	spen__	d, t, p
2	emble__	m, n, g
3	diff_rent	f, e, r
4	hist_ry	t, o, r
5	gover_ment	n, m, r
6	len_th	n, g, t
7	fin_lly	a, n, l
8	quan_ity	d, t, n
9	san_wich	n, a, d
10	valu_ble	b, a, u
11	su_prise	r, a, p
12	Feb_uary	b, r, v
13	reco_nize	k, a, g
14	pi_ture	c, t, sh
15	gra_itude	d, t, th
16	enviro_ment	m, n, d
17	lib_ary	r, b, v
18	fam_ly	b, i, l
19	wi_th	d, f, t
20	amb_lance	u, b, e

HEAR THE DIFFERENCE?
Primary or intermediate grades
Individual or group

Activity

Students fill in the letters which distinguish two words which have similar sounds from one another.

Preparation

Duplicate MAKEMASTER #46 for the appropriate grade level and give one copy to each child. If you prefer, make up and duplicate a similar worksheet using words from your own spelling list or from the Chapter Word List on page 68.

Procedure

1. Say one of the two words in the first box and have the children repeat the word.
2. Call on one child to spell the word aloud and then have all the children trace the correct word.
3. Then say the other word and follow the same procedure as above. (As you read the words in the boxes, be sure you vary the order in which you read the two words.)
4. Now repeat one of the words and ask the children to trace that word under its model, filling in the missing sound. Have one child spell the word aloud and ask all the children to check that they have spelled the correct word.
5. Then repeat the second word and have them follow the same procedure.
6. After you have followed this procedure for all of the paired words, ask the children to turn over their papers. Dictate the words in a random order and have students write them. Have them check and correct each word as you dictate the words by calling on one child to spell the word aloud.

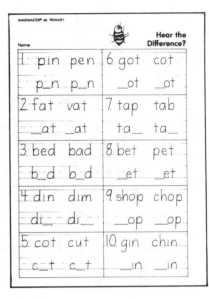

47

COVER THE PATTERN
Primary or intermediate grades
Individual or group

Activity

Students play a version of Bingo in which they use letter or letter combination markers to fill in the blanks in words on their Bingo playing cards.

Preparation

Make a grid similar to a Bingo card for each child. You will need to select a list of spelling words containing similar sounds which the children are having difficulty discriminating (such as *ou* and *au*). Write these letters on the grid cards, leaving out the troublesome letters or letter combinations. Place the words in a different order on each card. Laminate or cover the cards with clear adhesive paper so that you can use them repeatedly. Make a ditto of squares with one letter or one letter combination written on each square. Cut these apart so that each child has a set of word part squares to be used as markers. Each child will also need a piece of paper and pencil.

Procedure

1. Say the letter combination *ow*. Ask the children to repeat that sound and then to find their marker that has that sound on it.
2. Now say the first word *plow*. Ask the children to repeat it, locate that word square on their grid card, and place their marker there to complete the word.
3. Ask one child to say the word and spell it so everyone can check and correct before proceeding.
4. Follow this procedure until one child has covered the pattern you have designated (diagonal line, straight line, or letter shape).
5. Then take that child's card and ask the child to spell each word in the completed pattern.
6. After completing several rounds, have the children turn over their grid cards but keep their sound markers visible. Dictate the words, and have the children write them.
7. Have them turn over their grid cards to check and correct.

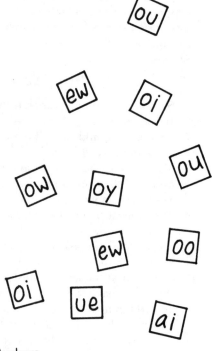

Markers

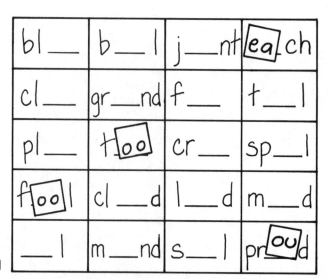

Playing card

 64 *Spell Well*

48

LETTER LIFT
Primary or intermediate grades
Individual or group

Activity

Students listen to dictated words, identify, and match the sounds heard with letter cards.

Preparation

After you select the similar sounds on which you want to focus (see the Chapter Word List on page 68 for examples of common discrimination errors), prepare a list of spelling words. Make a set of word cards large enough for all of the children to see clearly. Color code the sounds on which you are focusing. Cut out squares of tagboard. Write the sounds on the tagboard cards before passing them out or have the children write the letters on their own cards. Each child should have the same group of letter cards. Each child will also need a piece of paper and pencil.

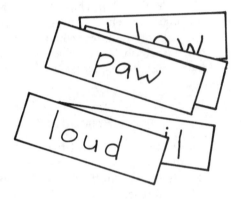

Procedure

1. Say the first word. Have the children repeat the word.
2. Then ask them to find and hold up the letter card that contains the sound(s) on which you are focusing in the word.
3. Next, hold up the large card showing the children the complete word. Check that everyone has chosen the card that matches the color coded sound. Then have them say the word again.
4. Remove the word card and ask the children to write the word.
5. Hold up the large word card again and have them check and correct.

Sounds cards

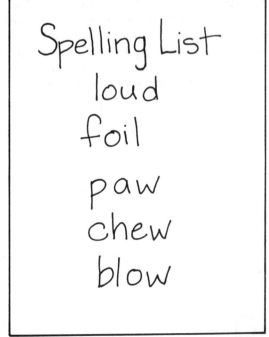

Spelling list

49

MAKE IT WHOLE
Primary or intermediate grades
Individual or group

Activity

Students differentiate between words having similar sounds by selecting the correct sounds to complete dictated words.

Preparation

Duplicate MAKEMASTER #49 for the appropriate grade level and give one copy to each child. Write the words to be dictated on the chalkboard. Here is a sample list which has been keyed to the MAKEMASTERS:

Primary: shin, chin; chop, shop; wish, witch; dish, ditch; rash, rich; ship, chip; wash, watch; shoe, chew; hash, hatch; chap, shape; mash, match

Intermediate: march, marsh; hush, hutch; rich, ridge; witch, wish; bash, batch; shoes, choose; lunch, lunge; wash, watch; shipper, chipper; bush, butch; badge, bash; shopper, chopper; hinge, hitch; crutch, crush

Procedure

1. Have the children read the words on the chalkboard. Then erase the words.
2. Say the sounds in the box at the top of the MAKEMASTER. Have the children repeat each sound carefully.
3. Say the first word on your list (*march*) and then say a sentence containing that word. Repeat the word in isolation again. Ask the children to choose the correct letter sounds to complete the dictated word and then fill in the blanks in the first word with their choice.
4. Ask one child to spell the word aloud. Then have all the children write the word on the blank next to the first word.
5. Say the second word on your list and follow the same procedure.
6. After completing the word list, have the children turn their papers over and dictate the words in a random order. Have them check and correct as you dictate the words by calling on one child to spell the word aloud.

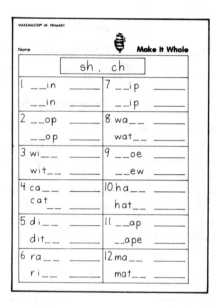

WHAT SHAPE IS IT IN?
Primary or intermediate grades
Individual or group

Activity

Students identify a spelling word when presented with the real word and a nonsense word shown in configuration.

Preparation

Duplicate MAKEMASTER #50 for the appropriate grade level and give one copy to each child. If you prefer, make your own worksheet using words such as those listed in the Chapter Word List on page 68. The words on each line of the sheet are enclosed to present two different shapes or configurations. One of the words is real, the other is a nonsense word with a similar sound.

Procedure

1. Have the children say aloud each word in the row. Explain that one is a spelling word and one is a nonsense word. Have them circle the real word.
2. When they have circled the real word in each pair, have them read their circled words to you.
3. Next, ask them to write the real word on the blank in column C to the right of each word pair.
4. Then tell them to turn their papers over and write the word again. Have them check and correct their spelling against the circled word.

Variation 1. Make a worksheet where only one shape is given per line and two words are written below it. Ask the child to write the correct word in the shape.

Variation 2. Make a worksheet in which you pair words with the same configurations which can be discriminated by different sounds, for example: ship and chip or drip and trip. Dictate one of the two words which have been paired. Ask students to listen carefully, then circle the word that you have dictated.

MAKEMASTER 50: PRIMARY

Name _____

What Shape Is It In?

	A	B	C
1	pan	pand	
2	fight	vight	
3	tribe	chibe	
4	those	vose	
5	dress	jress	
6	path	pash	
7	dis	this	
8	tob	top	
9	tooth	toof	
10	stuff	stuss	

MAKEMASTER 50: INTERMEDIATE

Name _____

What Shape Is It In?

	A	B	C
1	farther	varther	
2	transfer	chansfer	
3	entrust	enchrust	
4	bluff	bluth	
5	thunder	funder	
6	stirrup	stirrub	
7	expand	expan	
8	mush	muth	
9	thistle	fistle	
10	dropper	propper	
11	hinge	hinch	
12	sheriff	sheriv	
13	cherub	cherup	
14	avenue	afenue	

CHAPTER FIVE WORD LIST
Building Auditory Discrimination Skills for Spelling

PRIMARY

animal	fight	ship
bet	fought	shoe
black	got	shop
block	hash	shut
bomb	hatch	sought
bum	jut	this
cash	lunch	those
catch	mash	time
chain	match	tooth
chew	moon	top
chick	noon	train
chin	pan	tribe
chip	pen	vet
dime	pet	wash
dish	pin	watch
ditch	pit	went
dress	same	wish
fat	sane	witch

INTERMEDIATE

ambulance	gratitude	sandwich
avenue	grocery	several
banana	hinge	sheaf
bawl	history	sheath
bowl	hitch	sheriff
choose	important	shoes
chopper	interest	shopper
crush	lawyer	spend
crutch	lease	spent
dropper	leash	stirrup
emblem	leather	surprise
entrust	lengthy	thigh
environment	library	thistle
equipment	orange	thunder
family	picture	transfer
farther	popular	usually
favorite	probably	valuable
February	quantity	vegetable
final	recognize	vinyl
government	remember	width

PRIMARY AND INTERMEDIATE
Trouble Letters

a • o	i • e	t • d
b • g • d	n • m	tch • sh
ch • j	n • nd	th • f
dr • tr	o • u	th • sh
dr • gr	p • b	th • d
f • v	sh • ch	tr • ch
g • c	sh • j	any initial
g • ch	sh • ge • dge	vowel

GLOSSARY OF TERMS

answer key a means of making an activity self-correcting. You can put the answers on the back of the worksheet or on a separate paper for matching purposes.

auditorizing the important process of saying a word that you have written to yourself in order to monitor your spelling of the word. Many children who have difficulty with auditory discrimination have not learned to auditorize.

auditory discrimination the ability to hear similarities and differences between sounds within a word.

color coding a method for visually calling attention to the part of the word with which a child is having trouble (the "trouble spot"). You can do this by writing over the trouble spot in a bright color that makes it stand out.

configuration an outline of the perimetric shape of a word. Example: hang

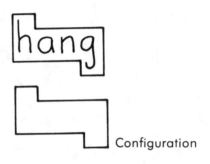

Configuration

diphthong two vowels which comprise one gliding, monosyllabic speech sound.

irregular or **nonphonetic** a word that is not pronounced the way that it is spelled.

liquid consonant a consonant whose sound is prolonged like that of a vowel; *r* and *l*.

mask a card or piece of paper used to cover any part of the worksheet you do not want a child to look at.

motor input muscular activities designed to introduce or reinforce other learning skills such as visual memory.

motor output muscular activities designed to demonstrate mastery or retention of other learning skills such as visual memory.

pocket chart a chart with slots or pockets for the insertion of activity cards.

position-in-space recognition the ability to perceive the position of a letter in relation to the observer's orientation in space.

revisualization the ability to remember the way a word looks and spell it in proper sequence.

sequencing the ability to recall letters and letter sounds in the correct sequence to spell a word.

visual discrimination the ability to differentiate the visual form of one letter from another.

visual memory the ability to remember accurately what has been seen in the past.

MAKEMASTER® DUPLICATABLE WORKSHEETS

Compare and See

Name

1. Correct spelling	2. Same or different?	3. S/D	4. Write it
saw	was		
stop	spot		
card	card		
from	form		
left	left		
won	won		
how	who		
name	name		
left	felt		
sag	gas		
snag	sang		
tap	tap		

Compare and See

Name

1. Correct spelling	2. Same or different?	3. S/D	4. Write it
under	undre		
head	haed		
kite	kiet		
become	boceme		
storm	strom		
farm	farm		
babies	babeis		
trunk	trunk		
friend	freind		
about	abuot		
teach	teach		
bright	bright		
goat	gaot		
fifty	fitfy		

Can You Tell the Difference?

Name

1.	
2.	
3.	
4.	
5.	
6.	
7.	
8.	
9.	
10.	
11.	
12.	
13.	
14.	

Name _____

Match the Box

how	was	who	saw
_ o w	w _ s	w _ o	s _ w
h _ w	_ a s	_ h o	s a _
h o _	w a _	w h _	_ a w
_ _ w	_ _ s	_ _ o	_ _ w
h _ _	w _ _	w _ _	s _ _
_ o _	_ a _	_ h _	_ a _
_ _ _	_ _ _	_ _ _	_ _ _

calm	mane	sang	felt
c a _ m	_ a n e	_ a n g	_ e l t
_ a l m	m a n _	s a _ g	f _ l t
c a l _	m _ n e	s _ n g	f e l _
c _ l m	m a _ e	s a _ _	_ e l _
_ _ l m	_ _ n e	_ _ _ g	f _ _ _
c _ _ _	_ _ _ e	_ a _ _	_ e _
_ _ _ _	_ _ _ _	_ _ _ _	_ _ _ _

Name _____

Match the Box

quiet	expect	quite	except
q iet	e pect	q ite	e cept
qu et	exp ct	qu te	ex ept
qui t	expe t	qu t	ex e t
q t	ex e t	q e	ex t
_____	_____	_____	_____

diary	aboard	dairy	abroad
d ary	ab ard	d ary	a road
d ry	ab rd	d ry	abr ad
di y	ab d	da y	abr d
d y	a d	d y	ab d
_____	_____	_____	_____

equipment	several	perform	their
e uipment	sev al	p form	th ir
e ipment	se al	perf m	the r
equi ment	sever	p f m	th r
equi men	s l	p m	t r
_____	_____	_____	_____

Watch the Order

Name

A	B			C
won	now	own	won	
tub	but	tub	ubt	
dog	god	dog	gdo	
girl	girl	gril	glir	
was	saw	aws	was	
eat	ate	eat	tea	
farm	fram	famr	farm	
who	who	how	ohw	
name	mane	name	nema	
clam	calm	clam	clma	
there	there	theer	three	
left	felt	letf	left	
stop	stop	spot	sopt	
tap	atp	tap	pat	

Watch the Order

Name

A	B			C
spread	spraed	spread	sapred	
forward	froward	forwrad	forward	
introduce	introduce	intorduce	intrdouce	
section	section	sectoin	seciton	
brief	breif	brief	brife	
listen	listne	lisetn	listen	
anxious	anxoius	anxious	axnious	
awful	awful	afwrul	awufl	
fifth	fifth	fitfh	fihtf	
ought	uoght	ought	ougth	
fabric	fabirc	fabric	fibrac	
quiet	quite	quiet	queit	
perform	preform	perfrom	perform	
except	expect	execpt	except	
probably	porbably	probably	probalby	
several	several	sverael	sereval	
dairy	dairy	diary	draiy	
bread	beard	bread	braed	
abroad	aboard	abraod	abroad	

Word Cut-Up

Name

Word list	Answer key
1. d o g	1. dog
2. t u b	2. tub
3. w a s	3. was
4. p a t	4. pat
5. e a t	5. eat
6 f r o m	6. from
7. s a n g	7. sang

Name

Word Cut-Up

Word list	Answer key
1. b a r n	1. barn
2. a n g e l	2. angel
3. a b o a r d	3. aboard
4. b r e a d	4. bread
5. c a r v e	5. carve
6. d a i r y	6. dairy
7. q u i e t	7. quiet
8. f i f t y	8. fifty
9. f r i e n d	9. friend

Spell Well copyright © 1980

Name

1.) A. The (clam) is (on) the (shore.)

B. The clam calm is on no the shroe shore.

C. The _____ is ___ the _____ .

2.) A. See the (little) (girl) (read.)

B. See the littel little gril girl read raed.

C. See the _____ ____ ____ .

3.) A. Look at (their) (blue) (desks.)

B. Look at thier their bule blue desks dseks.

C. Look at ____ ____ ____ .

4.) A. (Eat) (four) (apples) now.

B. Eat Ate fuor four apples appels now.

C. _____ ____ _____ now.

Make the Sentence Make Sense

Name

1. A. You must (usually) be (quiet) in a (hospital.)
   B. You must usually usaully be quite quiet in a hospital hopsital.
   C. You must _____ be _____ in a _____.

2. A. There are (probably) (several) good (performances.)
   B. There are probably probalby sevreal several good performances preformances.
   C. There are _____ _____ good _____.

3. A. That (fabric) (ought) to make a nice (spread.)
   B. That frabic fabric ought ouhgt to make a nice spraed spread.
   C. That _____ _____ to make a nice _____.

4. A. The (fifth) (section) should be (brief.)
   B. The fitfh fifth sectoin section should be brief breif.
   C. The _____ _____ should be _____.

5. A. (Listen) to the (train) and climb (aboard.)
   B. Litsen Listen to the trian train and climb abroad aboard.
   C. _____ to the _____ and climb _____.

6. A. (Expect) the (dairy) to have new (equipment.)
   B. Except Expect the dairy diary to have new equpiment equipment.
   C. _____ the _____ to have new _____.

Find the Hidden Letters

Name

A	B	C
bird	d(b)r x(i a(r)i b(d)r i a	b i r d
who	howoathweohwa	___
saw	awhsuwaswasom	___
club	dlabcdulbdudatb	____
their	hetiehblietiarhe	_____
first	trefrasithrtsitr	_____
tried	frtietretabidebd	_____
one	wneoaunmuwme	_____
stop	tosohzptotupsou	____
form	tmfarnoferofmat	____
clam	leamcantloenpamn	____
three	fratearheatrethe	_____
sang	grosngtamunpqgu	_____

Find the Hidden Letters

Name

A	B	C
dairy	a d i a y r d y i a r y d	dairy
perform	p r f e o r m f r o r m	
expect	e p x c p x e t c p t x e	
abroad	b a r b o r a o d a d	
equipment	i e u q u p i m p e m e n t	
fabric	a r f b r a b i r i a c	
quite	q i u i e t q e t u i	
except	e c p x p c t e t p t	
quiet	u i q t u i t e q t	
diary	r y d a i r y a r y	
aboard	a o b r d o r a r b d	
poise	s p i s e o p i e s e	
hospital	h o p s i p t i a t l a l	
several	v s a e v r e a r e a l	
usually	u s a u l y a l l a y	
bread	r b e a r d e r a b d e	

Name

Say It Slowly

1. desk deks ————	5. on no ————
2. girl gril ————	6. stop spot ————
3. was saw ————	7. from form ————
4. tap pat ————	8. who how ————

Say It Slowly

1. desk deks _____	10. glutton gulton _____
2. perpare prepare _____	11. children childern _____
3. expect except _____	12. secretary secertary _____
4. quiet quite _____	13. government govrenment _____
5. popular poplar _____	14. popluation population _____
6. reforce reinforce _____	15. important inportant _____
7. substance sustance _____	16. broad board _____
8. insturment instrument _____	17. ornament ormanent _____
9. dupilcate duplicate _____	18. aminal animal _____

Listen and Write

Name _____

1. grab garb _____ grad drag	6. tires tried _____ tied tired
2. stop step stay _____ spot	7. cats cast calls _____ stack
3. paste pats _____ pals play	8. felt feel flit _____ fell
4. grid girl grip _____ grill	9. then three there _____ tree
5. best bets step _____ sets	10. name mane man _____ none

Listen and Write

1. thrifty
   thirsty
   thirty

   _____

2. abroad
   aboard
   abound

   _____

3. particular
   practical
   particle

   _____

4. hospital
   hospitable
   hospitality

   _____

5. exception
   expectation
   exemption

   _____

6. quickly
   quietly
   guilty

   _____

7. dairy
   diary
   dreary

   _____

8. pious
   poise
   posies

   _____

Spell Well copyright © 1980

What's My Shape?

Name _____

A	B	C
talk _alk t_lk t__k ⎯ ⎯ ⎯ ⎯		1. _ _ _ _ _
said s_id _aid sa__ ⎯ ⎯ ⎯ ⎯		2. _ _ _ _ _
many man_ _any __ny ⎯ ⎯ ⎯ ⎯		3. _ _ _ _ _

89

Watch Out for Silent Letters

Name

1. could	
2. lamb	
3. talk	
4. night	
5. often	
6. know	
7. sign	
8. high	
9. write	
10. walk	
11. light	
12. would	
13. bright	

Name

Watch Out for Silent Letters

| 1. comb |
| 2. gnome |
| 3. daughter |
| 4. psalm |
| 5. climb |
| 6. height |
| 7. wrestle |
| 8. condemn |
| 9. gnat |
| 10. halves |
| 11. castle |
| 12. delight |
| 13. pneumonia |
| 14. listen |
| 15. gnaw |
| 16. through |
| 17. tongue |
| 18. balked |
| 19. knowledge |
| 20. answer |

Name

Spell It Now

s	a	i	d
c	o	m	e
w	a	n	t
d	o	e	s
s	o	m	e
t	h	e	y
w	e	r	e

Name

dif	fer	ent	
trans	por	ta	tion
fa	vor	ite	
quan	ti	ty	
ne	ces	si	ty
rea	son	a	ble
rec	og	nize	
en	vi	ron	ment
no	tor	i	ous
de	li	cious	

Seven Steps to Success

Name

Words to Learn	Step 1 Say word.	Step 2 Write word in syllables.	Step 3 Spell word aloud.	Step 4 Close eyes. Spell word.	Step 5 Write word without looking at model.	Step 6 Check and correct	Step 7 Repeat

Name

What Am I?

Sentences	Answers
1. All of the boys go to school and then th_y go home.	4. **any**
2. Mary w_s playing with me last week.	6. w**o**rk
3. Tommy likes to ta_k to his cat.	9. goes
4. Do you have _ny apples to eat?	7. bri**gh**t
5. I think I _now how old you are.	1. th**ey**
6. He has fun doing w_rk in the yard.	3. ta**l**k
7. The bri__t sun shines all day.	2. w**a**s
8. Sam s__d he had to go home to eat.	5. **k**now
9. Mary go__ to the pool to swim.	10. clim**b**
10. Can you clim_ up the tree to get the cat down?	8. s**ai**d

What Am I?

Name

Sentences	Answers
1. The old man lit a huge cig_r.	7. ancient
2. There is more than one relig__n in the world.	10. giraffe
3. When a person has the flu, they sometimes have a bad co___.	2. religion
4. In high school, the s_ience class is one of the most important.	11. thimble
5. Does your stom___ hurt after eating too much?	1. cigar
6. Do you have tr__ble with spelling?	8. group
7. The anc__nt statue was crumbling with age.	4. science
8. To what singing gr__p do you belong?	6. trouble
9. A begg_r sat on the street with a cup in his hand.	12. machine
10. What a long-necked gira__e we saw at the zoo.	5. stomach
11. Thumbelina was as small as the size of a thimb__.	3. cough
12. The incredible ma__ine was working beautifully.	9. beggar

Name _____

Color Clue

Trace	Write		Write
1. worm	_____		1. _____
2. would	_____		2. _____
3. two	_____		3. _____
4. does	_____		4. _____
5. want	_____		5. _____
6. other	_____		6. _____
7. believe	_____		7. _____
8. color	_____		8. _____
9. little	_____		9. _____
10. their	_____		10. _____
11. white	_____		11. _____
12. watch	_____		12. _____
13. very	_____		13. _____

Name

Color Clue

Trace	Write		Write
1. build	_____	1.	_____
2. women	_____	2.	_____
3. poison	_____	3.	_____
4. young	_____	4.	_____
5. bicycle	_____	5.	_____
6. museum	_____	6.	_____
7. because	_____	7.	_____
8. bargain	_____	8.	_____
9. recognize	_____	9.	_____
10. guard	_____	10.	_____
11. eager	_____	11.	_____
12. toward	_____	12.	_____
13. cousin	_____	13.	_____
14. bracelet	_____	14.	_____

Programmed
Spelling Practice

Name

	A	B	C
	sup sap	pir per	_____ _____
	sup	per	_____
	thim thin	bul ble	_____ _____
	thim	ble	_____
	gop gob	lun lin	_____ _____
	gob	lin	_____
	brais brace	let lut	_____ _____
	brace	let	_____
	cig sig	nul nal	_____ _____
	sig	nal	_____
	sun son	shin shine	_____ _____
	sun	shine	_____
	trap tarp	ease eze	_____ _____
	trap	eze	_____

Break It Up

Name

Spelling words	Number of syllables		Whole word
1.			
2.			
3.			
4.			
5.			
6.			
7.			
8.			
9.			
10.			
11.			
12.			
13.			
14.			
15.			

Type It Out

Name

again
animal
been
busy
come
does
friend
love
one
two
who
were
your

Type It Out

Name

acre
anxious
athlete
bicycle
colonel
guard
knife
language
onion
picnic
precious
rhythm
sugar
toward
twelve
villain
women
young

Find the Odd Ball

Name

1. b b b b d b b b b b b b b b	
2. n n n n n n n n u n n n n n	
3. z z z z z z z z z z z s z z z z	
4. g g g g g g g g g g g g g g	
5. s s s s s s s s e s s s s s s s s s	
6. d d d d p d d d d d d d d d	
7. big big dig big big big	
8. mad map mad mad	
9. saw saw saw was saw	
10. gun gun qun gun gun	
11. beak peak beak beak	

Name

Count It Up

1. b d b p q b d d p p q	
2. n u m n n u m m u u	
3. v w v w w v u w n	
4. d b b b b d d d b d b	
5. h y h h n y y h u n y	
6. n u u n u n n n n u u	
7. p g p p g g p g p p g	
8. b d p q g y b d g y q b	
9. g q g q g g p q d q	

MORE

Count It Up

Name

10. dry pry dry bry	
11. bat bat pat dat	
12. mad map mad mad	
13. got qot got got	
14. boh boy boy boh	
15. run rnu ruu run	
16. saw sav saw sav	
17. pig pip pig pig	
18. nut rut nut hut	

Trace Your Steps

Name

b	b b d p d b q b d p b	
d	d b d d p q d b d a b	
p	p q g g p q b p g q d p	
q	q q g g p q p g g p p q	
b	b d g d b d d b b g p d	
d	d b d d b d p b g b g b d	
n	n u m n n u u m n u n u n	
u	u n n u u m n u n u m u n	
g	g g q q p p g g g a b g p q	

MORE

Trace Your Steps

Name

be	be de b pe be	
jut	jut jut jut jut	
pig	pig dig big pig	
up	up np ud up up	
go	go po qo go go	
dad	dad bad dad	
pad	pad paq pab pad	
ban	ban pan ban dan	
gap	gap gag pag gap	

Name

Trace Your Steps

1. plaid	plaid plaib dlaid plaid	
2. money	money money mouey money	
3. queen	queen queen queen queen	
4. broad	broad droad broad broab	
5. guide	guide guide quide quibe	
6. delight	delight belight delight belight	
7. past	past qast past dast	
8. debt	debt bebt bedt debt	
9. babble	babble dabble baddle badble	
10. wiggle	wiggle miggle wiggle wigqle	
11. guilty	guilty quilty giulty guilty	
12. bugle	bugle dugle bugle dugle	
13. quilt	quilt quilt quilt quilt	
14. blond	blond dlond blond blonb	
15. guild	guild guild guild quilb	
16. bridge	bridge bribge dribge bridge	

Matchmakers

Name

feel	fell	map	nap
feel	fell	map	nap
ran	ram	girl	grill
ran	ram	girl	grill
jog	joy	fill	till
jog	joy	fill	till
cat	oat	bat	hat
cat	oat	bat	hat

Name

Match and See

a	a o d a a d b a o a d	-----
i	i j l i i j j i i l i l j i i l j	-----
h	h b n h h b n h h n b	-----
y	y g g y y p y g h y g y	-----
v	v w m v w w v w m v v	-----
f	f t t f f t f t f f f t t f	-----
it	if if it if it it ti if	-----
ran	ram ran ran ram rau	-----
vine	vine wine wine viue	-----
oat	oat cat aot cat oat	-----
fan	tan fan fan fun tan	-----
puff	putt puff put puff	-----

Match and See

Name

m	m m n w m m m n m	
f	l l f b f f b j l b f f l f	
e	e e l e i e e l e e i l e e	
u	u w u u v v u w u u n	
j	f j j i j b f i j f f j j i j	
l	l e f f l l e l e f l l e l	
chimp	chimp chinp chinp chimp	
joined	joined foined joimed joined	
feeler	feller jeeler feeler feleer	
loose	loose lose lose loose	
every	every ever very every	
attack	attach attack attach attack	
simple	sinple single simple simgle	
thirty	thrifty thirty thrifty thirty	
filth	filth fifth filth fifth	
angle	angel angle angle angel	
chose	choose chose chose choose	
curtain	certain curtain curtain certain	
odor	odor order odor order	
insisted	insisted instead insisted	
even	ever evem even even ever	
hotel	hostel hotel hostel hotel	
mummy	mummy munny mummy	
pebble	pebfle peffle pebbel pebble	

Name

 Look Carefully

1. A. nut

B. The squirrel ate a large $^{nut}_{hut}$

C. The squirrel ate a large____.

2. A. run

B. I like to $^{rum}_{run}$ very fast.

C. I like to ___very fast.

3. A. tan

B. You can get a good $^{tan}_{fan}$ at the beach.

C. You can get a good___at the beach.

4. A. boy

B. Go and ask that $^{bog}_{boy}$ to help you.

C. Go and ask that____ to help you.

5. A. feel

B. A warm bath will $^{fell}_{feel}$ good.

C. A warm bath will ____ good.

Look Carefully

Name _____

1. A. ankle B. The athlete sprained his ~~angle~~ ankle. C. The athlete sprained his _____.
2. A. chose B. He ~~choose~~ chose five members for the team. C. He _____ five members for the team.
3. A. odor B. The blossoms have a pleasant odor ~~order~~. C. The blossoms have a pleasant _____.
4. A. attach B. We will ~~attack~~ attach the strings to the kites. C. We will _____ the strings to the kites.
5. A. certain B. Are you certain ~~curtain~~ that is the man you saw? C. Are you _____ that is the man you saw?
6. A. thrifty B. It pays to be a ~~thirty~~ thrifty shopper. C. It pays to be a _____ shopper.
7. A. every B. He always completes every ~~even~~ homework assignment. C. He always completes _____ homework assignment.
8. A. farther B. Mr. Smith must travel ~~father~~ farther than Dad. C. Mr. Smith must travel _____ than Dad.
9. A. instead B. She asked for fried potatoes instead ~~insisted~~ of mashed. C. She asked for fried potatoes _____ of mashed.

Look Alikes

Name

1. cot cat cof caf col cat	-------
2. fan tam fon tan fam fan	-------
3. bat bof baf hat hat bal	-------
4. silt sift sitt sift siff	-------
5. aat cat act oat aot oat	-------
6. name nane nome name mane	-------
7. ever even ewer euer even	-------
8. noom none noon nome noon	-------
9. vet wet wef wet vef wel	-------
10. feet fell feel fell feef	-------
11. happy bappy baggy happy	-------
12. nome home hone home none	-------

Look Alikes

Name _____

1. farther father fartler farther	_____
2. thritty thrifty thirty thrifty	_____
3. very every even ever every	_____
4. attach aftach attack attach	_____
5. insisted instead imsisted instead	_____
6. odor order ordre order orber	_____
7. lifth fifth filth fifth fibth	_____
8. simple sinple single simple simple	_____
9. joim join goim join joen foin	_____
10. loose lose eoose losee loose	_____
11. thirst therst thirft thirst first	_____
12. curtain certain curfain curtain	_____
13. enblem emblem emblen emblem	_____
14. lusler luster lwster luster twster	_____
15. elevator ellvator elevator eelvator	_____
16. whlee wheel whell vheel wheel	_____

Name

Close the Gap

1. sp_t   i, a, o

2. fle__   sh, ch

3. p_n   i, a, e

4. to_   t, b, p

5. t_ck   i, e, u

6. lun__   ch, sh

7. _ace   f, th, v

8. ca_   p, t, b

9. w_nt   i, e, u

10. __at   th, f, v

11. _olt   d, th, t

12. __ain   tr, ch

13. __ink   dr, tr

14. p_t   e, i, o

Name

Close the Gap

1. spen__	d, t, p	
2. emble__	m, n, g	
3. diff__rent	f, e, r	
4. hist__ry	t, o, r	
5. gover__ment	n, m, r	
6. len__th	n, g, t	
7. fin__lly	a, n, l	
8. quan__ity	d, t, n	
9. san__wich	n, a, d	
10. valu__ble	b, a, u	
11. su__prise	r, a, p	
12. Feb__uary	b, r, v	
13. reco__nize	k, a, g	
14. pi__ture	c, t, sh	
15. gra__itude	d, t, th	
16. enviro__ment	m, n, d	
17. lib__ary	r, b, v	
18. fam__ly	b, i, l	
19. wi__th	d, f, t	
20. amb__lance	u, b, e	

Spell Well copyright © 1980

Name

Hear the Difference?

1. pin pen p_n p_n	6. got cot _ot _ot
2. fat vat _at _at	7. tap tab ta_ ta_
3. bed bad b_d b_d	8. bet pet _et _et
4. din dim di_ di_	9. shop chop _op _op
5. cot cut c_t c_t	10. gin chin _in _in

Spell Well copyright © 1980

Name

Hear the Difference?

1.	black bl___	block bl___	8.	vinyl _inyl	final _inal
2.	same s___	sane s___	9.	chin __in	shin __in
3.	chick ch___	check ch___	10.	chump __ump	jump __ump
4.	jell __ell	shell __ell	11.	time __ime	dime __ime
5.	shut __ut	jut __ut	12.	sheaf shea__	sheath shea__
6.	hutch hu___	hush hu___	13.	bowl b___	bawl b___
7.	shack __ack	jack __ack	14.	stock st___	stuck st___

Name _____

Make It Whole

sh , ch

1. __ __ in _____ __ __ in _____	7. __ __ ip _____ __ __ ip _____
2. __ __ op _____ __ __ op _____	8. wa __ __ _____ wat __ __ _____
3. wi __ __ _____ wit __ __ _____	9. __ __ oe _____ __ __ ew _____
4. ca __ __ _____ cat __ __ _____	10. ha __ __ _____ hat __ __ _____
5. di __ __ _____ dit __ __ _____	11. __ __ ap _____ __ __ ape _____
6. ra __ __ _____ ri __ __ _____	12. ma __ __ _____ mat __ __ _____

Make It Whole

Name _____

ch, tch, sh, ge, dge

1. mar___ ___ ___
   mar___ ___

2. hu___ ___
   hu___ ___

3. ri___ ___
   ri___ ___

4. wi___ ___
   wi___ ___

5. ba___ ___
   ba___ ___

6. ___oes ___
   ___ oose ___

7. lun___ ___
   lun___ ___

8. wa___ ___
   wa___ ___

9. ___ipper ___
   ___ipper ___

10. bu___ ___
    bu___ ___

11. ca___ ___
    ca___ ___

12. ___opper ___
    ___opper ___

13. hin___ ___
    hi___ ___

14. cru___ ___
    cru___ ___

What Shape Is It In?

Name

A	B	C
1. pan	pand	– – – – – – –
2. fight	vight	– – – – – – –
3. tribe	chibe	– – – – – – –
4. those	vose	– – – – – – –
5. dress	jress	– – – – – – –
6. path	pash	– – – – – – –
7. dis	this	– – – – – – –
8. tob	top	– – – – – – –
9. tooth	toof	– – – – – – –
10. stuff	stuss	– – – – – – –

What Shape Is It In?

Name

A	B	C
1. farther	varther	
2. transfer	chansfer	
3. entrust	enchust	
4. bluff	bluth	
5. thunder	funder	
6. stirrup	stirrub	
7. expand	expan	
8. mush	muth	
9. thistle	fistle	
10. dropper	jropper	
11. hinge	hinch	
12. sheriff	sheriv	
13. cherub	cherup	
14. avenue	afenue	